/ t

Si s

Maya Angelou

tes y Imelda Pilgrim

York Press

YORK PRESS
322 Old Brompton Road, London SW5 9JH

ADDISON WESLEY LONGMAN LIMITED
Edinburgh Gate, Harlow,
Essex CM20 2JE, United Kingdom
Associated companies, branches and representatives throughout the world

First published 1998

ISBN 0-582-36831-6

Designed by Vicki Pacey, Trojan Horse, London
Illustrations by Julian Page
Map by Celia Hart
Phototypeset by Gem Graphics, Trenance, Mawgan Porth, Cornwall
Colour reproduction and film output by Spectrum Colour
Produced by Addison Wesley Longman China Limited, Hong Kong

C ONTENTS

PREFACE

York Notes are designed to give you a broader perspective on works of literature studied at GCSE and equivalent levels. We have carried out extensive research into the needs of the modern literature student prior to publishing this new edition. Our research showed that no existing series fully met students' requirements. Rather than present a single authoritative approach, we have provided alternative viewpoints, empowering students to reach their own interpretations of the text. York Notes provide a close examination of the work and include biographical and historical background, summaries, glossaries, analyses of characters, themes, structure and language, cultural connections and literary terms.

If you look at the Contents page you will see the structure for the series. However, there's no need to read from the beginning to the end as you would with a novel, play, poem or short story. Use the Notes in the way that suits you. Our aim is to help you with your understanding of the work, not to dictate how you should learn.

York Notes are written by English teachers and examiners, with an expert knowledge of the subject. They show you how to succeed in coursework and examination assignments, guiding you through the text and offering practical advice. Questions and comments will extend, test and reinforce your knowledge. Attractive colour design and illustrations improve clarity and understanding, making these Notes easy to use and handy for quick reference.

York Notes are ideal for:
- Essay writing
- Exam preparation
- Class discussion

The author of these Notes is Imelda Pilgrim, a full-time teacher of English in a comprehensive school in the North East of England. She is the author of the York Notes on *Roll of Thunder, Hear My Cry*. She is an English graduate and a Principal Examiner for English for a major GCSE examination board.

The text used in these Notes is the Virago 1996 edition of *I Know Why the Caged Bird Sings*.

Health Warning: **This study guide will enhance your understanding, but should not replace the reading of the original text and/or study in class.**

PART ONE

INTRODUCTION

HOW TO STUDY A NOVEL

You have bought this book because you wanted to study a novel on your own. This may supplement classwork.

- You will need to read the novel several times. Start by reading it quickly for pleasure, then read it slowly and carefully. Further readings will generate new ideas and help you to memorise the details of the story.
- Make careful notes on themes, plot and characters of the novel. The plot will change some of the characters. Who changes?
- The novel may not present events chronologically. Does the novel you are reading begin at the beginning of the story or does it contain flashbacks and a muddled time sequence? Can you think why?
- How is the story told? Is it narrated by one of the characters or by an all-seeing ('omniscient') narrator?
- Does the same person tell the story all the way through? Or do we see the events through the minds and feelings of a number of different people?
- Which characters does the narrator like? Which characters do you like or dislike? Do your sympathies change during the course of the book? Why? When?
- Any piece of writing (including your notes and essays) is the result of thousands of choices. No book had to be written in just one way: the author could have chosen other words, other phrases, other characters, other events. How could the author of your novel have written the story differently? If events were recounted by a minor character how would this change the novel?

Studying on your own requires self-discipline and a carefully thought-out work plan in order to be effective. Good luck.

Maya Angelou, a black American writer, was born named Marguerite Johnson in 1928 in St Louis, Missouri (see Map of States on p. 8 for position of places). Her parents soon divorced and she was sent, with her brother Bailey, to her paternal grandmother in the segregated southern state of Arkansas where she spent much of her childhood. During a visit to St Louis when she was eight years old, she was raped by her mother's boyfriend. She did not speak for five years after this traumatic event.

In 1940, Maya Angelou moved to San Francisco with her mother and, whilst attending High School, she became pregnant and gave birth to a son in 1945. In 1952, she received a scholarship to study dance in New York and then joined the European tour of *Porgy and Bess*. When she was thirty Maya Angelou moved to New York, joined the Harlem Writers' Guild and became involved in the Civil Rights Movement. She moved to Egypt where she edited *Arab Observer* and then to Ghana where she was feature editor of *African Review* and taught at the University of Ghana. From 1959 to 1960, at the request of Martin Luther King Jr., she served as the Northern Co-ordinator for the Southern Christian Leadership Conference. In 1974, she was appointed by Gerald Ford to the Bicentennial Commission and later by Jimmy Carter to the Commission for International Woman of the Year.

She speaks several languages and has been awarded numerous honorary degrees and awards for her work in literature, film and television. In addition to her prose writings she is a renowned poet. In 1993, Maya Angelou became the first woman and first African-American to read a poem for the Presidential inauguration. This poem, *On the Pulse of Morning*, won immediate acclaim and earned her a Grammy award for Best Spoken Word.

I Know Why the Caged Bird Sings was published in 1970 and is an account of Maya Angelou's childhood up to the birth of her son. It is the first of five volumes of **autobiography** (see Literary Terms).

CONTEXT & SETTING

Much of the novel takes place in the southern state of Arkansas in the 1930s and is set against a background of racial distrust and disharmony. To understand the writer's experiences and point of view you need to have some understanding of the historical background.

Civil War   The United States of America is formed from a number of states (see Map on p. 8), each of which has its own laws about internal matters. Federal laws, however, are fixed by the President and Congress and apply to all states. In the period prior to the Civil War enormous differences had developed between the northern, more industrialised states, and the southern agricultural ones, which relied heavily on slave labour, the slaves having been originally imported from Africa in the seventeenth century.

In 1861 the Civil War began. Whilst the main aim of the North was to restore the Union, broken by the formation of the Confederate States of America in 1860, a secondary aim was to free all slaves. The war was long and bitter, continuing until 1865, when the southern Confederacy surrendered to the northern general, Ulysses Grant.

Reconstruction   There followed a period of racial adjustment, known as *and the*   Reconstruction (1865–77), which was imposed by the *Ku Klux Klan*   North on the South. During this time slavery was abolished and four million Blacks were granted freedom. This was resented by southern Whites, who still believed that Blacks were fundamentally inferior.

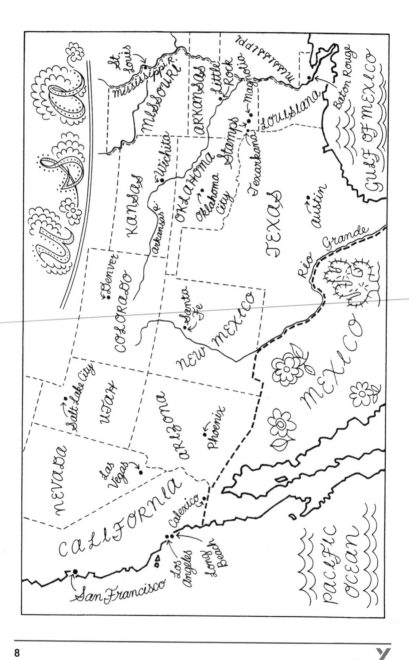

One product of this resentment was the formation of the Ku Klux Klan in 1866. This was a secret society whose primary aim was to re-establish white supremacy. It is fear of the Klan, referred to as 'the boys', which forces Uncle Willie to hide in a bin as described in Chapter 3. Maya's views on the Klan are also made clear in this chapter.

Racial hatred Reconstruction was followed by a period of fear and intimidation for black people in the South. Many of the laws that had made them equal were rejected and reversed, and between 1882 and 1903 over 2,000 black people were lynched and many terrible atrocities were committed. Though the story is set in the 1930s, the fear that such a reign of terror generated is still evident in Momma's belief that white folks could not be talked to 'without risking one's life' (p. 46, Chapter 7). Bailey experiences this hatred of some Whites for Blacks in Chapter 25 when a black man's body is pulled from the pond. It is after this incident that Momma moves the children back to their mother. The North, whilst still carrying many racist attitudes, offered Blacks more freedom and opportunity. Maya, for instance, is able to attend, and indeed thrives at, the George Washington High School which has a predominantly White intake (Chapter 28).

The Depression In the 1930s America was hit by a serious economic depression, started by the Wall Street Crash in 1929. The South was hit very badly by this, with the price of cotton falling dramatically. The effect of the Depression on the Negro community is described in Chapter 8. The price paid for a pound of cotton dropped from ten to five cents, forcing many families onto Welfare.

The Second World War In 1941 the Japanese attacked Pearl Harbor, the American naval base in Hawaii, bringing the United States into the Second World War. The effect of this on the Japanese living in San Francisco is clearly recorded in Chapter 27, where Maya writes of how they disappeared 'soundlessly and without protest' (p. 204) to be replaced by Blacks newly arrived from Georgia and Mississippi (see Map of States on p. 8).

Equality for all

In addition to understanding the historical events, which form the background to *I Know Why the Caged Bird Sings*, it is useful to recognise the later influences on the writer's life. In her thirties Maya Angelou became involved in the Civil Rights Movement. This started in 1954 as an attack on racial segregation in the southern states but quickly broadened to encompass racial subordination in all areas of life. Led by Martin Luther King Jr., who was assassinated in 1968, the movement had an enormous impact in the United States. Maya Angelou's involvement in this at a high level, combined with her equally strong desire to promote and fight for women's rights, is evident throughout her writing. It is little wonder that, when considering the plight of the young black female, she considers her to be 'caught in the tripartite crossfire of masculine prejudice, white illogical hate and Black lack of power' (p. 265, Chapter 34).

PART TWO

SUMMARIES

GENERAL SUMMARY

The story traces the early unsettled years of the author, Maya Angelou, when she and her brother, Bailey, were moved between their mother in San Francisco, California and their grandmother in Stamps, Arkansas. The first separation from their parents, caused by the breakdown of their marriage, came when Maya was only three years old. The trauma was eased by the presence of Bailey, the older by one year and the most important person in her young life.

Chapters 1–8: Stamps

In Stamps the children live with their paternal grandmother, Momma, and the disabled Uncle Willie. They are well cared for and raised in a strict but loving environment. As the years pass, Maya grows in her respect and love for Momma, a strong, determined, God-fearing woman who successfully manages a business during the Depression and always maintains an air of humility. Maya recalls with pride how she was once referred to as 'Mrs' by a judge and how she withstood the taunts of a group of white girls, ultimately gaining a subtle victory over them. Uncle Willie is a somewhat distant figure, a man who takes pride in his appearance and who, very conscious of his disability, once pretended to be able-bodied.

These early years are filled with a series of fragmented recollections of people and incidents. Much of the detail is set against the background of the Store, which Momma owns, a place of comfort and security in Maya's childhood. There she meets the cotton pickers and sees the harsh realities of their lives and it is there that Uncle Willie hides in a bin following Mr Steward's warning that the Ku Klux Klan would be riding that night. The fear of the Klan and the distrust of Whites in general is a recurring theme. Maya, on her occasional excursions into the white part of town, considers them to be almost alien beings.

Maya recalls significant people outside her immediate family such as Mr McElroy, a Black distinguished by his independent status, and the Reverend Thomas, hated by both herself and Bailey, who was humiliated in church one Sunday at the hands of the eccentric Sister Monroe.

Always in the background is the sense of displacement (see Theme on p. 63) and insecurity brought about by the children's early separation from their parents. When presents from their parents arrive unexpectedly one Christmas, both Maya and Bailey are deeply distressed. At the age of seven Maya's world is turned upside down by the arrival of her handsome and gregarious father. To her he is a stranger and Maya is upset to learn that she and Bailey are to return with him to California.

Chapters 9–13: St Louis

For the next six months they live with their mother's family in St Louis, Missouri. The Baxters, with the powerful, pale-skinned grandmother and five wild uncles, are notorious for their tempestuous 'flamboyant escapades' (p. 64, Chapter 10) and close family bonds. The children's mother, Bibbi, is the only girl, and both Bailey and Maya are struck by her beauty. After six months the children move in with her, spending much of their time in the care of her boyfriend, Mr Freeman. Maya is sexually abused by Mr Freeman and when she is eight years old she is raped by him. This, the subsequent trial, and the murder of Mr Freeman have a devastating effect on the young child, creating overpowering feelings of guilt and shame. In consequence she resolves to speak to no-one except Bailey. Shortly afterwards the children are sent back to their grandmother in Stamps.

Maya's self-imposed silence continues until, through the gentle encouragement of Mrs Flowers, a friend of Momma's, she starts to gain in confidence and her early love of reading flourishes. When she is ten she goes to work for Mrs Cullinan and her independent spirit is clearly demonstrated when, insulted by Mrs Cullinan renaming her 'Mary', she smashes the best kitchenware and leaves the house.

Chapters 14–24: Stamps again

Both she and Bailey continue to feel confusion at the separation from their mother and this is brought to the fore when Bailey sees a film in which the lead actress looks like her. Nevertheless, the Stamps community offers a welcome refuge from the pain of the past and Maya recalls, in detail, events such as the revival, the radio broadcast of the World Championship boxing match and the summer picnic. It is at the latter event that she makes her first friend, Louise Kendricks. Not long after, Bailey falls in love with Joyce, who later runs off with a railroad porter, an episode which marks the gradual loosening of the bonds between the children.

At twelve Maya graduates and a glorious day is overshadowed by the speech of Mr Edward Donleavy, who talks about the degradation and humiliation of the Negro race. The day is saved, however, by Henry Reed who leads the hall in the singing of the Negro national anthem. The prejudice and racist attitudes of the Whites is reinforced by Maya's visit to Dr Lincoln, the white dentist who refuses to treat Maya, and by Bailey's experience of hatred and contempt when a black man's body is pulled out of the pond. It is at this point that Momma decides to take both children back to California.

Chapters 25–29: California

They stay in Los Angeles (see Map on p. 8) for several months, Momma making a remarkable adjustment to life in this alien city before returning to Stamps and leaving the children to go to San Francisco with their mother. Maya's admiration for her mother grows, not least because of her ability to stand up for herself, clearly demonstrated when she shoots her working partner for calling her a bitch. She is also fond of her mother's husband Daddy Clidell, and learns much about life and card-games from him and his friends. Growing to love San Francisco, she feels at home there despite the constant presence of racism. At school she is inspired by the teaching of Miss Kirwin and at fourteen she gains a scholarship.

Chapters 30–36: Father and mother

Maya spends a summer with her father and his girlfriend, Dolores, in southern California. She does not get on well with Dolores who clearly feels threatened by her presence. One week Maya's father takes her to Mexico (see Map on p. 8) with him and there she sees a completely different side to him as he mixes familiarly with the Mexicans. After a hair-raising journey home, when Maya drives because her father is drunk, they are greeted by the furious Dolores, who subsequently stabs Maya. Though she is treated for her injuries, she decides to run away and spends a month living rough in a junk-yard. She learns much from this experience before finally returning to her mother.

Maya is feeling increasingly unsettled and out of step with her peers. When Bailey leaves home after an argument with their mother she decides to get a job on the San Francisco streetcars. With determined forcefulness, and the unstinting support of her mother, she is successful and becomes the first Negro to work on the streetcars.

Her return to school some months later prompts a curiosity about her own sexuality. She decides to seduce a boy on her street and discovers three weeks later that she is pregnant. It is only after she has achieved her High School diploma and when she is six months pregnant that her mother and stepfather learn of her condition. Her son is born three months later and, despite her initial fears, a close bond is formed between them.

DETAILED SUMMARIES

PREFACE

In what ways does Maya lack self-confidence?

The story begins with an incident in the Colored Methodist Episcopal Church. It is Easter Sunday and Marguerite (henceforward referred to as Maya), unable to recall the words of a particular poem, is being laughed at by the other children. She is wearing the dress her grandmother had made for her. She had thought it beautiful but now she sees it as plain and ugly, revealing her skinny legs and shading her skin the colour of mud. She longs for the day when her true white self will be revealed. In an attempt to avoid further embarrassment she leaves the church, tripping over as she does so. Unable to hold on any longer she starts to wet herself and runs home. Her sense of humour overtakes her and she begins to laugh, filled with a sense of freedom and relief.

COMMENT

The writer's lack of self-confidence and sense of insecurity as a child is made plain to the reader. She describes her physical appearance as being unattractive and reveals a strong desire to become a white girl. This shows how racist attitudes have filtered down to her even as a child.

The words of the poem she recites are important as her self-consciousness and the lack of a permanent home are significant features of her formative years.

The dark mood of this opening section is lifted temporarily by Maya's ability to laugh at herself and her own misfortunes.

The last two sentences of the Preface set the scene, and establish the main subject of the novel.

GLOSSARY   **angel's dust** a smile

green persimmon the unripe fruit of the tropical persimmon tree

CHAPTER 1

Maya is separated from her parents when she is three years old

With the break-up of their parents' marriage, three-year-old Maya and her four-year-old brother Bailey are sent to live with their paternal grandmother in the town of Stamps in the southern state of Arkansas. Their grandmother, whom the children call Momma, lives with her son, Willie, and owns the successful Wm. Johnson General Merchandise Store in the middle of the black area of Stamps.

As the years pass Maya becomes familiar with the routines of the cotton pickers, who buy their provisions in the Store in the early hours, before they are loaded onto wagons to be transported to the cotton plantations. The mornings were filled with optimism about how much cotton would be picked that day, but the evenings were slow, sad times when the pickers realised their efforts would never be enough to pay their debts. Having seen the harsh realities of their existence, Maya acknowledges that in later life she was to be angered by the stereotyped picture of the happy, singing cotton picker.

COMMENT

Much of Maya's insecurity in later years stemmed from this early separation from her parents as a result of the break-up of their marriage.

From the very beginning the grandmother is portrayed as a strong and determined character who has built up a successful business from a mobile lunch counter.

Notice the combination of childhood memories and the adult viewpoint.

Through her memories of the cotton pickers and the harshness of their lives, the writer makes clear that childhood influences and experiences were to have a very strong effect on her adult life and the development of her thinking.

GLOSSARY **economic promises** promises made by the North to the black population following the American Civil War, in the period known as Reconstruction

slavery's plantations the huge farms on which the cotton is grown and which, at one time not long ago, were run on slave labour

fo' bits and six bits small amounts of money

white commissary a shop supplying food and/or equipment

vittles Americanised spelling of the English word 'victuals' which means food provisions

CHAPTER 2 At five years old Maya and her brother, Bailey, are trained in their times tables by Uncle Willie, with threats of harsh punishment if they make a mistake.
Why does Uncle Their uncle is crippled as the result of an accident when
Willie pretend to he was three years old. Maya recalls some of the
be able-bodied? difficulties he experienced and how once, when strangers visited the Store, he pretended not to be lame. He stood without his walking stick and, whilst Maya did not understand his need to do this, it made her feel very close to him.

During her early childhood Maya develops a passion for Shakespeare, identifying with the ideas expressed therein. She read widely but was never able to admit to Momma that her favourite playwright was a white man.

COMMENT The sense of being presented with a series of significant 'snapshots' from childhood is very evident in this account of Uncle Willie's pretence to be able-bodied. Maya appears to identify strongly with his struggle to achieve something that was important to him, despite the difficulties involved.

From an early age Maya's love of literature is evident. The problem over Shakespeare suggests that Momma

would have banned her from reading the works of a
white writer.

GLOSSARY   **Kipling, Poe, Butler, Thackeray and Henley** English writers
            **Paul Lawrence Dunbar, Langston Hughes, James Weldon Johnson
            and W.E.B. Du Bois** black American writers

CHAPTER 3   The Store itself is a significant place to the young
            Maya. She finds satisfaction in doing her jobs correctly

The Store   and punishes herself when she makes mistakes. It is a
provides a place that is full of promise in the morning, tired in the
sense of   afternoon and comforting in the evening.
security

Why does Uncle   Both she and Bailey have their regular daily jobs, one of
Willie have to   which is to feed the pigs. One evening they are
hide?   disturbed by the arrival of Mr Steward, the one-time
                   sheriff, who has come to warn Momma that the Klan
                   would be riding that night. Maya remembers the
                   intense fear she felt on hearing this and the way
                   Momma immediately set to hiding Uncle Willie in a
                   bin below layers of onions and potatoes. He moaned so
                   loudly that he would almost certainly have been
                   discovered had the Klan appeared.

As an adult, Maya recalls the harshness of the faces of
the Klan members and her inability to accept that they
had ever been young. She is unable to feel any gratitude

towards Mr Steward for his warning, because of the arrogance with which it was delivered.

COMMENT   The description of the Store evokes a strong sense of belonging and security, emphasising its importance to Maya. Maya often **personifies** (see Literary Terms) it in her description.

The actions of Momma and Uncle Willie, on hearing the Klan would be riding, reflects the extent to which they feared them.

The adult writer's dislike of the Klan is made clear, as is her resentment against the humiliation caused to her and her family by Mr Steward's warning.

GLOSSARY   **skillets** flattish pans used in cooking, like a frying-pan
nigger a derogatory word used to describe a black person
The 'boys' a reference to the members of the Klan
the Klan the Ku Klux Klan, a secret society whose main aim was to enforce white supremacy

CHAPTER 4   Maya argues that the home town has a significant influence over later experiences of life. Mr McElroy was a neighbour of theirs and unusual in that he did not go to church and was seemingly independent, an almost unique status for a Black at that time. He is a mystery to the young Maya and an object of fascination, though her adult years brought about the realisation that he was not a particularly interesting man.

The most important person in her young world is, without question, her brother Bailey. He is her hero, handsome, articulate, athletic, mischievous and good fun. To emphasise his importance in her life she describes him as her 'Kingdom Come' (p. 23).

A significant custom in Stamps was the preservation of meat after the killing season which followed the first frost. Momma is helped in this by her neighbours,

STAMPS

and the family live on the smoked food throughout the year.

Maya regards Whites as alien beings

Twice yearly, however, she and Bailey are sent to buy liver in 'whitefolksville' (p. 24). Blacks rarely entered this area and for Maya it was a frightening experience. She records her impressions of the Whites at that time and her feeling that they were not quite real, so marked were the divisions between the two parts of the population.

COMMENT

Notice the **episodic** (see Literary Terms) nature of the chapter. We are told about Mr McElroy, as though he were a significant character, and yet he does not appear later in the story.

Why does she describe Bailey as her 'Kingdom Come'?

The importance of Bailey in Maya's childhood is shown clearly. She regarded him with a kind of hero worship and he was undoubtedly the most influential figure in her childhood.

The complete divide between black and white is vividly illustrated in Maya's journey across town and in her perception of white people as being alien and unreal.

GLOSSARY

weevils small, grub-like creatures which commonly inhabit rice and flour meal

my Kingdom Come reference to the next world or life after death

CHAPTER 5

In the winter Maya has to wash in ice-cold water in compliance with her grandmother's insistence on cleanliness. Obedience was essential and there were strict rules on how children should address adults. Maya states that these were obeyed by all except the children from poor white families, some of whom live on the land owned by Momma. Despite their poverty, the colour of their skin gives these 'powhitetrash' (p. 27) children the power to be rude to both Momma and Uncle Willie.

One morning a group of white girls arrive at the Store,
whilst Maya is raking the yellow-red dust in the yard
with Momma looking on admiringly. Maya is sent
inside but Momma remains outside. The children start
to ape Momma's posture and make fun of her whilst
she continues to stand still, quietly humming the tune
of a hymn. Finally, having failed to get a reaction from
Momma, one of the girls does a handstand, insultingly
revealing her nakedness below her dress. Momma
remains motionless and, as the girls leave, she says
goodbye to each of them using the title Miz. Maya is,

What victory does at first, infuriated by her humility but soon realises that
Momma gain? Momma has scored some kind of victory. She comes
out and reworks the dust into a heart shape, much to
Momma's satisfaction.

COMMENT   The writer cites this incident as the starting point of a
lifelong preoccupation, presumably referring to her
subsequent feelings about the treatment and inequalities
suffered by Blacks at the hands of Whites.

By remaining silent and unmoved by the incident
Momma gives the girls no satisfaction and defeats their
attempts to ridicule her. Had she been abusive to them
she would almost certainly have suffered for it.

clabbered milk curdled milk
powhitetrash derogatory term for poor and ill-mannered Whites
roustabout derivation from cowboy slang; now generally used to
indicate daring, impudent, outspoken behaviour
cat-o'-nine-tails an instrument of punishment, a stick with nine
leather thongs
molasses-slow molasses is raw sugar; in liquid form it is like
golden syrup and flows very slowly

CHAPTER 6   Both Bailey and Maya hate Reverend Howard Thomas
who stays with them on his quarterly visits to the
church. Not only is he obese and fails to remember
their names but he ruins Sunday breakfast and eats the

best part of Sunday dinner. The advantage of his visit is that, by listening secretly to the adult conversation, the children learn of all the latest scandals in the area.

The children's sense of humour gets them into trouble　One morning Maya and Bailey were sitting in church while Reverend Thomas was preaching. Sister Monroe is there, who had previously caused havoc by shouting out loudly '"preach it"' (p. 38) and grabbing hold of Reverend Taylor. On this particular morning she interrupts his sermon in the same way. The children are unable to withhold their laughter as the scene before them becomes increasingly chaotic and Reverend Thomas's false teeth are sent flying, landing by Maya's foot. Their laughter stops only when Uncle Willie appears, cane in hand. The children receive such a severe whipping that the minister's wife asks Uncle Willie to quieten them.

COMMENT　Religion plays a central part in the children's upbringing. They are raised strictly and their expected standard of behaviour is sharply contrasted against the behaviour of the white girls in the previous chapter.

Maya's sense of fun is strongly evident in this chapter and she and Bailey are able to laugh freely together (until fiercely whipped).

GLOSSARY　**Gladstone** British statesman, Prime Minister four times
Deuteronomy the fifth book of the Old Testament
Pharisees ancient Jewish sect associated with self-righteousness and hypocrisy
Mount Nebo mountain in Egypt from which Moses viewed the Promised Land

CHAPTER 7　Momma is an unusual woman in many respects. Married three times, Maya recalls the Saturday night when her third husband turns up. He stays until Sunday and then leaves, having been prevented from stealing by the watchful eye of Uncle Willie.

Momma is referred to as 'Mrs' Henderson in court

Maya remembers her grandmother as a powerful and strong person and sees evidence of this in the way she sings at church every Sunday with both sincerity and humility. She teaches the children the ways she has found to be safe, advising total caution in any dealings with white people. She takes great pride in having once been referred to as 'Mrs' Henderson by a judge in court, who mistakenly believed that only a white woman could own a store. This raised Momma's status in the neighbourhood.

COMMENT

Maya has huge respect and even awe for her grandmother, though from an adult standpoint is able to question her beliefs and actions.

How does the use of a person's title demonstrate respect?

The fact that a white judge would not normally refer to a black woman as 'Mrs' demonstrates an enormous lack of respect. The assumption that only a white woman could own a store reflects the general poor economic and social standing of the Blacks.

GLOSSARY

George Raft American film star (1895–1980) with gangster connections
chifforobe a wardrobe

CHAPTER 8

The black community suffers from the Depression

Despite the deep-rooted prejudice against Blacks, Maya, as a child, feels a grudging admiration for the Whites' lifestyle. She is impressed by their material possessions but is puzzled by what she regards as their wastefulness. In contrast Momma makes the children's clothes and only Uncle Willie has ready-to-wear clothes.

The area is hit badly by the Depression and the Blacks suffer when the price for a pound of cotton drops from ten cents to eight to eventually five. Momma manages to keep her business going and her family off relief by exchanging credit for welfare provisions.

Why are the children upset?

One Christmas the children receive presents from their parents. Up to this point Maya had convinced herself that they were dead. Both she and Bailey are deeply upset by the arrival of the gifts. Neither child has come to terms with their abandonment and both shoulder feelings of guilt and worthlessness. They decide the presents could be a sign that their mother is preparing to have them back.

COMMENT The contrast between the wealth of the white community and the poverty of the black draws attention to the unfairness and inequality that existed.

The Depression had a devastating effect on both the white and the black communities, hitting the latter hardest about two years after its start.

Momma's ingenuity and business sense are clearly demonstrated by the way she manages to keep the Store going despite the Depression.

The confusion and bewilderment of the children surfaces painfully with the arrival of their parent's presents.

GLOSSARY **Chitlin' Switch, Georgia; Hang 'Em High, Alabama; Don't Let the Sun Set on You Here, Nigger, Mississippi** invented stereotypical towns in southern states notorious for their racist attitudes – see Map of States on p. 8
July Fourth the day of the adoption of the Declaration of Independence in 1776; otherwise known as Independence Day
the Depression serious economic depression of the 1930s started by the Wall Street Crash in 1929

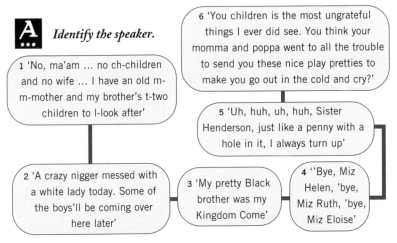

A *Identify the speaker.*

6 'You children is the most ungrateful things I ever did see. You think your momma and poppa went to all the trouble to send you these nice play pretties to make you go out in the cold and cry?'

1 'No, ma'am ... no ch-children and no wife ... I have an old m-m-mother and my brother's t-two children to I-look after'

5 'Uh, huh, uh, huh, Sister Henderson, just like a penny with a hole in it, I always turn up'

2 'A crazy nigger messed with a white lady today. Some of the boys'll be coming over here later'

3 'My pretty Black brother was my Kingdom Come'

4 ''Bye, Miz Helen, 'bye, Miz Ruth, 'bye, Miz Eloise'

Identify the person(s) 'to whom' this comment refers.

7 Fate not only disabled him but laid a double-tiered barrier in his path. He was also proud and sensitive

8 Boys? It seemed that youth had never happened to them. Boys? No, rather men who were covered with graves' dust and age without beauty or learning

9 She did an excellent job of sagging from her waist down, but from the waist up she seemed to be pulling for the top of the oak tree across the road

Check your answers on page 88.

B *Consider these issues.*

a The way you are presented with a series of episodes rather than a continuous story.

b The way the adult viewpoint is sometimes imposed on the childhood memory.

c How Bailey and Maya are both affected by the early separation from their parents.

d The importance of Momma and Uncle Willie in providing the children with a stable and secure home.

e What you have learned so far about the way Blacks were treated by Whites.

f How the children's parents have behaved towards them.

CHAPTER 9

The children meet their parents

When Maya is seven her father arrives unexpectedly. She is filled with admiration for this big, handsome stranger who has his own car and speaks 'Proper English' (p. 53). During the three weeks of his stay many people visit him at the Store, full of curiosity. Maya is filled with confusion, feeling unnerved by her father's presence and uncertain about the future. She is shocked to learn of his intentions to take Bailey and herself with him when he leaves and considers refusing to go. Though saying little, Momma is clearly saddened by the loss of the children.

On the journey Maya learns that she is going to her mother's and is terrified. In desperation she speaks to Bailey in Pig Latin only to find she is understood by her father who is much amused by her fears.

When she meets her mother she is in awe of her beauty. She notes with wariness that Bailey has instantly forgotten all the loneliness of his childhood and fallen in love with their mother. His reaction makes her feel even more lonely and isolated. Their father leaves a few days later. To Maya he is still 'a stranger' (p. 59), as is her mother.

COMMENT

The insecurities of the children and their sense of abandonment comes to the fore as they face the momentous meeting with their mother.

How does Bailey's response differ to Maya's?

Maya initially perceives her parents in terms of their physical attractiveness. She seems afraid of her father's intrusion into her life, partly because she dreads the time when it will end.

GLOSSARY

sun perch and striped bass common species of fish

Pig Latin a secret language used by children

CHAPTER 10

What are your first impressions of Maya's mother's family?

For the next six months the children live in the house of their maternal grandparents. The Baxters are well known in St Louis, notorious for their toughness. There were six children: five boys and Bibbi, the children's mother. Grandmother Baxter, though of Negro origin, has white skin and is a powerful figure in the criminal fraternity. Her position as 'precinct captain' (p. 60) gives her influence with the police department. When Maya's mother was cursed by Pat Patterson, her brothers cornered him in a saloon and invited her to hit him. She did, leaving him almost dead. There was no police investigation following this incident.

Besides becoming accustomed to the ways of their new family, the children have much to learn about life in St Louis. Maya grows to love some of the new foods she experiences, though both children find the students of their age at school surprisingly backward. They are put in a higher class and Bailey takes delight in displaying his superior knowledge. Maya learns from her uncles that she received her name from Bailey when she was very young, who, refusing to call her Marguerite, referred always to her as '"mya sister"' (p. 66) which was later shortened to 'Maya'.

The children sometimes visit their mother at work at the tavern Louie's. They learn to dance and experience at first-hand their mother's power over men. After six months they move in with her. They are still haunted by the fear of being sent back to Stamps if they misbehave. Their mother lives with Mr Freeman, an older man who was, in Maya's eyes, lucky to have got her.

COMMENT

Are there other similarities between the grandmothers?

One of the main reasons for the widespread respect for Maya's grandmother was the paleness of her skin. Like Momma she is also a powerful and resilient woman.

Maya's mother's family is very close and mutually supportive. They believe that violence is a viable way of settling difficulties.

Maya's mother is portrayed as a very glamorous figure, who the children worship from a distance.

GLOSSARY

quadroon a person who is one quarter Negro

octoroon a person having one quadroon and one white parent

Victrolas old-fashioned record players

slaw coleslaw

siditty this probably comes from the word 'acidity' and indicates a sharp tongue

didoes games, pranks

CHAPTER 11

Mr Freeman plays on Maya's insecurity and need for affection

The children are frequently left in the care of Mr Freeman. They continue to feel insecure and Bailey develops a stutter while Maya has nightmares. On one occasion, after sleeping in her mother's bed because of a nightmare, Maya is sexually abused by Mr Freeman. She does not understand what is happening and finds the closeness with which he holds her comforting. She is even more puzzled when Mr Freeman accuses her of having wet the bed and threatens to kill Bailey if she tells anyone what has happened. This is the first secret Maya has ever kept from Bailey. After a further incident of abuse Mr Freeman stops speaking to Maya. She is hurt and confused by this, but as the months pass is no longer bothered by it.

COMMENT   Maya's innocence and naïveté is clearly demonstrated in these disturbing accounts of abuse. Her longing for physical comfort is not surprising in a child who has received so little.

The account suggests that Mr Freeman tries to fight his impulses by avoiding Maya, thus adding to the confusion and hurt experienced by the child.

CHAPTER 12

The trauma of rape   At the age of eight Maya is raped by Mr Freeman. After the violence of the act he tells her to act normally and again threatens to kill Bailey if she tells anyone what has happened. In extreme pain, Maya walks to the library and is close to collapse by the time she returns home. The following days pass in a blur of fever, pain and confusion. She becomes aware that Mr Freeman has left after an argument with her mother, but it is not until Bailey and her mother change the bed that her soiled underwear is discovered and the reason for her condition becomes apparent.

COMMENT   The clarity with which the writer recalls this dreadful violation of herself as a child helps the reader to

Why does Maya feel guilty?   understand its full horror and to enter into the confusion of a child's mind. Not only does she not understand what has happened to her but she feels guilty and frightened as well.

CHAPTER 13

Maya retreats into silence Maya is taken to hospital. She tells Bailey who raped her, believing his assurances that the man will not kill him. She then has to face the ordeal of the trial. When asked if Mr Freeman had touched her before the rape she is faced with a terrible choice – whether to tell the truth and risk the wrath of her family towards her or to lie when under oath. Reluctantly she chooses to lie. Mr Freeman is sentenced to a year and a day but is released from prison that afternoon. Later a policeman visits the Baxter household to tell them that Mr Freeman has been kicked to death. Maya, convinced that this is the direct result of her lie and unable to cope with the feelings of guilt or to confide in Bailey, resolves to speak to no one apart from her brother. Her concern that other people might die if she speaks remains with her and her voluntary silence is at first a cause for concern and then a source of irritation to her family. Eventually both she and Bailey are sent back to Stamps and Maya never discovers whether this is because of her silence or because her grandmother sent for them.

COMMENT Again the mind of the child is clearly revealed to the reader. Misunderstandings create even more pain and misery for a child who has already suffered too much.

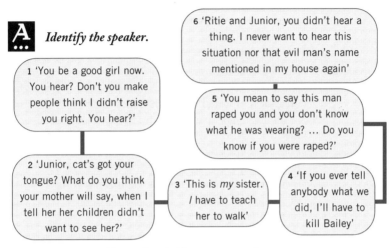

A *Identify the speaker.*

1 'You be a good girl now. You hear? Don't you make people think I didn't raise you right. You hear?'

2 'Junior, cat's got your tongue? What do you think your mother will say, when I tell her her children didn't want to see her?'

3 'This is *my* sister. *I* have to teach her to walk'

4 'If you ever tell anybody what we did, I'll have to kill Bailey'

5 'You mean to say this man raped you and you don't know what he was wearing? ... Do you know if you were raped?'

6 'Ritie and Junior, you didn't hear a thing. I never want to hear this situation nor that evil man's name mentioned in my house again'

Identify the person(s) 'to whom' this comment refers.

7 She was like a pretty kite that floated just above my head

8 I admit that I was thrilled by their meanness. They beat up whites and Blacks with the same abandon, and liked each other so much that they never needed to learn the art of making outside friends

9 He leaned over, his whole face a threat that could have smothered me

Check your answers on page 88.

B *Consider these issues.*

a The reasons for Maya's anxieties about going to St Louis.

b What we learn about the closeness of the Baxter family and the ways they support each other.

c How Mr Freeman is portrayed, in some respects, as a man to be pitied.

d The way the writer conveys the horror of the rape and the innocence of a young child.

e The contrast between the glamorous Bibbi at work and the concerned mother tending her sick child.

f How you are made aware of Maya's confusion and guilt during the trial.

CHAPTER 14

Maya returns to a safe place   Maya is relieved to return to Stamps where both she and Bailey are accepted back into the community with a great deal of initial curiosity. Bailey takes great pleasure in telling the people wonderful made-up stories about life in the North, which gain him the admiration of both Momma and Uncle Willie. Maya continues with her self-imposed silence, and at times worries for her own sanity, but the people of Stamps regard her unwillingness to talk as an indication of how much she misses the big city.

COMMENT   Back at Stamps Maya finds a degree of peace and acceptance that had not been available to her in St Louis.

GLOSSARY   **King's English** standard English, as thought to be spoken at court

CHAPTER 15

In what ways does Mrs Flowers help Maya?   Maya's life continues with little change for the best part of a year, until she is taken under the wing of Momma's friend, Mrs Flowers. Maya greatly admires this thin, neatly dressed gentlewoman and is embarrassed by Momma's casual way of talking to her. She is delighted when Mrs Flowers asks that she, rather then Bailey, should carry her provisions from the Store. After the fleeting humiliation of having to undress to display Momma's skill at needlecraft, Maya accompanies Mrs Flowers home and is delighted to be lent some books. Mrs Flowers encourages Maya to read aloud, explaining that it is the human voice that gives words their meaning. She rushes home with left-over cookies for Bailey and brims with delight and confidence, knowing she is liked by Mrs Flowers. Her

Is Momma's response to Maya's language fair?   elation is short-lived, as Momma, hearing her say 'By the way' and believing this to be blasphemous, makes her pray for forgiveness on her knees and hits her with the switch.

COMMENT   Maya has much to learn from Mrs Flowers about herself and others. Her pleasure in the knowledge that she is liked by Mrs Flowers shows the extent to which her self-image has been shattered by the rape.

As a child she did not think that Momma may have asked Mrs Flowers to speak to her, though with adult eyes she now considers this likely.

GLOSSARY   **Jesus was the Way, the Truth and the Light** Christian belief; Maya's use of 'By the way' was interpreted by Momma as a violation of this

CHAPTER 16

Maya rebels against unfairness and seeks revenge   When Maya is ten she is sent to work in the home of Mrs Viola Cullinan, a white woman from Virginia, and is fascinated by the precision of routine with which the house is run. The work is shared with Miss Glory, the cook, who has been in Mrs Cullinan's service for many years. Maya feels sorry for Mrs Cullinan, who could not have children and whose husband has fathered two daughters by a coloured woman. Maya determines to work as hard as she can to help compensate for her loss.

One evening one of Mrs Cullinan's visitors suggests that 'Margaret', Mrs Cullinan's incorrect pronunciation of 'Marguerite', should be shortened to 'Mary'. The next day Mrs Cullinan calls her 'Mary'. Maya is hugely insulted by this and not comforted by Miss Glory's information that her real name was 'Hallelujah'. She decides to quit the job as soon as possible and deliberately drops some of the best kitchenware in full view of Mrs Cullinan. As she leaves the house in uproar, she hears Mrs Cullinan refer to her as 'Margaret'.

COMMENT   Maya's kindly and sympathetic nature is demonstrated in her initial response to Mrs Cullinan's plight.

This episode shows the arrogance and smugness of the Whites who believed it was acceptable to change a servant's name simply on a whim and the pretension of convenience.

It also shows Maya's determination not to accept such treatment. She is of a different generation to Miss Glory and fights back in a dramatic and effective way.

GLOSSARY   tureen deep, circular, earthenware dish

CHAPTER 17

Bailey stays out late

On Saturdays many families stop at the Store on their way to town. It is Maya's favourite day even though she has more chores to do. She usually gives her weekly ten cents to Bailey, who likes to go to the movies. One night Bailey does not come home until late and offers no reason for this, despite a severe beating from Uncle Willie. Maya realises that something has affected him deeply and later learns that he had seen a white movie star who looked like their mother and had stayed to watch the film again. Two months later they both go to see the same film star. Maya is delighted by the similarity, but Bailey remains upset and terrifies Maya when he dashes out in front of the night freight train. She mentions in passing that a year later he caught a freight train in search of his mother, but ended up stranded in Baton Rouge, Louisiana (see Map of States on p. 8) for a fortnight.

COMMENT   The effect of the film on Bailey shows his insecurity and the extent to which he misses his mother, with whom he fell in love at first sight.

Maya's response is in sharp contrast to this; she is simply proud that her mother should look like a white movie star but be even prettier.

CHAPTER 18

Religion plays   After a hard day's work the cotton pickers stop off at
a central part   the Store on their way home. Maya is angered by their
in the life of   humble acceptance of their situation. One particular
the black   evening she learns that, in spite of their exhaustion,
community   they are going to get cleaned and go to the church for
the revival. For them this was an opportunity to feed the soul rather than the body.

The revival is held in a cloth tent in the middle of a field and is attended by people from many different denominations. It develops into a lively and emotional meeting which gives hope to the people and rekindles their belief in the justice and righteousness of God. Looking back, Maya sees how the people believed what they wanted and needed to, in order to make the suffering and humiliation of their own lives bearable.

COMMENT   The irritation Maya feels, even as a child, with the cotton pickers' uncomplaining acceptance of their difficult lives sheds light on her own feelings and actions in later life.

The importance of religion in the lives of these people is clearly demonstrated. It provides the basis of their belief system and the confidence and spiritual support to get them through each difficult day.

GLOSSARY   **two-by-fours** lengths of wood with a rectangular cross-section
revival religious festival intended to produce a reawakening of faith
Holy Rollers religious fanatics who roll on the floor in ecstatic experience
First Corinthians a book of the New Testament
John Brown US abolitionist leader (1800–59), hanged after leading an unsuccessful rebellion of slaves

CHAPTER 19

A black man becomes World Champion

A fight between Joe Louis, the black champion of the world, and a white boxing opponent draws the crowds to the Store to listen to Uncle Willie's radio. Details are listened to anxiously as each blow received by the black fighter represents yet another blow against the Negro race. His final triumph is regarded as a victory for black people, giving both delight and pride to those listening in the Store. Those with long journeys choose to remain in the town, rather than face the perils of the journey on a night when a Black had been victorious over a White.

COMMENT   The sense of community is strongly conveyed in this chapter as the people gather together to listen to the fight, all sharing the same hopes and fears.

How do you think the Whites felt?   This is more than just a fight between two men. It symbolises the conflict between Blacks and Whites in which, for once, the Blacks are victorious.

GLOSSARY   **Baby Ruths** a type of sweet
R. C. Colas, Dr. Peppers, and Hire's root beer different kinds of drinks
Joe Louis/Brown Bomber US boxer and world heavyweight champion

CHAPTER 20

Maya finds a friend

The summer picnic is a major event in the year's calendar, attended by representatives of all the churches and social groups. There is music, food and the children spend the time playing games. Maya wanders off into a small clearing, where she is joined by Louise Kendricks, a girl her age who she admires and in whom she senses loneliness. They talk and play together and Maya is impressed by her ability to 'fall in the sky' (p. 137). Louise becomes Maya's first friend and together they learn the difficult Tut language.

At school Maya receives her first Valentine from Tommy Valdon. Confused by his intention Maya tears the note up, only to receive another at school the following day. She is unable to stop giggling whenever she sees him and eventually he gives up his pursuit of her.

COMMENT

Again the community is a focal point with the summer picnic attended and enjoyed by all.

In what ways are Maya and Louise similar?

Maya's need for isolation and her unwillingness to play with the other children is made clear, as is the significance of her finding a friend.

Maya's confusion over the Valentine perhaps stems, to a large extent, from her traumatic sexual experience and the association of this with the suggestion of love.

GLOSSARY

chow-chow a relish made up of various things including mixed pickles

CHAPTER 21

Bailey falls in love

At the age of ten Bailey is becoming more sexually aware. His innocence is demonstrated in the pretend games he plays until he meets Joyce. She is four years older than him and makes an immediate conquest, her sexual experience being made apparent the first time Bailey invites her into his tent. Despite Maya's warnings Bailey falls in love with Joyce, stealing things from the Store for her to show the strength of his affection.

A stranger to the area from the start, Joyce disappears as quickly as she had appeared, causing great distress to Bailey. Months later Maya learns that she had run away to Texas (see Map of States on p. 8) with a railroad porter. When Maya tries to talk to Bailey about this he closes the conversation bluntly and her name is not mentioned again.

COMMENT   Both children are becoming increasingly sexually aware, though Maya's past experience continues to have a strong effect on her.

Puberty forces a distance between Maya and her brother, as Bailey becomes increasingly introvert, refusing to share his thoughts with her.

GLOSSARY   **Captain Marvel** heroic, comic-strip character
show fare small items, very often edible, bought at a fare
blood will tell family characteristics will surface

CHAPTER *22*

Maya hears a ghost story

One stormy night the family are unexpectedly disturbed by Mr George Taylor, a neighbour and recent widower. He is invited to join them in their evening meal. Maya is disturbed by the expression in his eyes. Maya had gone to Mrs Taylor's funeral at the insistence of her grandmother and had been deeply affected by the service and the sight of Mrs Taylor's body. As Momma expresses sympathy for Mr Taylor, the loss of his wife and his childlessness, he suddenly becomes agitated and tells of how his wife had spoken to him the previous night.

Mr Taylor insists he had been visited by a baby angel and had heard his wife say that she wanted some children. Gripped with fear, Maya is horrified to be sent on an errand to the kitchen and her superstitious mind makes this a terrifying expedition. As Momma tries to rationalise and find an explanation for Mr Taylor's experience, normality returns. Maya lays a pallet for Mr Taylor to sleep in and she is grateful for the company of Momma in the bed that night.

COMMENT

What opinions have you formed of the black community so far?

This is a community where people care for each other. Momma is one of many to have fed Mr Taylor since his wife's death.

Maya's vivid imagination is clearly illustrated in this childhood recollection and she attributes her belief in ghosts to her 'super-religious Southern Negro grandmother' (p. 161).

GLOSSARY   **Br'er Rabbit rag doll** a character in the *Uncle Remus* stories, tales based on black folklore by Joel Chandler Harris. Brer Rabbit was an animal endowed with human qualities

hoedown a lively dance

CHAPTER 23

Graduation is an important event in the community, marking a shift between childhood and adult responsibility. At twelve, Maya is graduating from the eighth grade with a top place. Momma has made her a new dress and she receives presents from neighbours and family, including the collection of poems by Edgar Allan Poe from Bailey.

The day has a dreamlike quality, though by evening Maya is feeling nervous. Her confidence is restored by the sight of her school friends. Unease sets in, however, when the choir director fails to follow the American national anthem and pledge of allegiance with what Maya refers to as the Negro National Anthem. She detects anxiety in the principal's voice, which is explained when the guest of honour, the white Mr *Why might Mr* Edward Donleavy, starts to speak. Whilst superficially *Donleavy have* praising the children's achievements, his speech is filled *spoken in this way?* with contempt. Made to face the inequalities of the education system, Maya feels a sense of hopelessness for the future of her race. All pride in her achievement is lost and, as she receives her diploma, she is filled with unhappiness and resentment.

The situation is saved, however, by the valedictory address of Henry Reed. Veering from his planned speech he turns to the graduating class and leads them in the singing of the Negro National Anthem. The audience join in and for the first time Maya hears the true significance of the words and her pride in herself and her race is restored.

COMMENT   Maya takes pride in her academic achievements and is growing in self-confidence. It is important to her that this occasion is shared with her family.

The importance of graduation to the community shows
the emphasis it places on education. Mr Donleavy's
speech exposes the inequalities of the education system
whereby all resources are focused on the white school.

Maya despairs, not only at the injustice with which the
Blacks are treated, but also with their apparent inability
to fight back.

Whilst reflecting on the achievements of the Negro
race, Maya pays tribute to the inspirational work of its
poets, preachers, musicians and blues singers.

GLOSSARY   **the Constitution** statute embodying the principles on which the
                  US is governed
                  Booker T. Washington Booker Taliaferro Washington
                  (1856–1915), an educationist, born a Mulatto slave who
                  became an important spokesman for black rights
                  The Rape of Lucrece a Shakespeare play which recounts the
                  story of a Roman noblewoman who stabbed herself to death
                  after being raped
                  *Gabriel Prosser and Nat Turner leaders of slave uprisings in
                  Virginia, striving for freedom. They were both eventually
                  hanged.
                  *Abraham Lincoln sixteenth president of the US – famous for
                  saving the Union in the Civil War and for the emancipation of
                  slaves
                  Emancipation Proclamation the law passed by President Lincoln
                  to banish slavery and free all slaves in the 1860s
                  *Harriet Tubman (1821–1913), a slave who was hit with a hoe
                  on her head when she was a young girl. She eventually
                  escaped to Virginia and helped a further three hundred slaves
                  escape. One of her jobs was working as a conductor on an
                  underground railroad
                  *Christopher Columbus Italian navigator and explorer who
                  discovered the New World
                  Santa María the boat in which Christopher Columbus had
                  travelled to the New World
                  James Weldon Johnson a black American writer, poet and lawyer

All characters indicated by * are well-known figures in American history whose public actions Maya wished had been other than they were

CHAPTER 24

Dr Lincoln refuses to treat Maya

Maya has toothache and is in severe pain. Momma takes her to Dr Lincoln, the white dentist in Stamps, to whom she had previously lent money. When they arrive Maya is ashamed to hear Momma refer to herself as 'Annie' to the white receptionist. She asks Dr Lincoln if he will treat Maya. He refuses, at first choosing his words carefully but becoming increasingly angry as Momma persists in her efforts. Finally he says that he would rather put his hand inside a dog's mouth. Momma tells Maya to wait downstairs. She imagines Momma ordering the dentist to leave Stamps immediately and him being extremely scared of her powerful words. When Momma joins her she tells her they are going to Dentist Baker in Texarkana (see Map of States on p. 8). They do so and Maya is treated and freed of her pain. Later Maya discovers Momma got the money to pay for the journey by charging Dentist Lincoln ten dollars interest on the loan which had originally been given freely. Momma is pleased with her achievement, but Maya wishes her imagined conversation had been true.

COMMENT

Momma's care for Maya is clearly demonstrated by her willingness to try everything to help her when she is in pain.

How do you feel about what Dr Lincoln says?

The blatant racism of Dr Lincoln is shown in the ferocity of his words to a woman who has helped him in the past.

GLOSSARY   **peckerwood dentist** derogatory slang meaning a white dentist

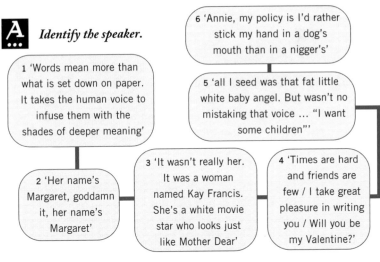

A *Identify the speaker.*

6 'Annie, my policy is I'd rather stick my hand in a dog's mouth than in a nigger's'

1 'Words mean more than what is set down on paper. It takes the human voice to infuse them with the shades of deeper meaning'

5 'all I seed was that fat little white baby angel. But wasn't no mistaking that voice ... "I want some children"'

2 'Her name's Margaret, goddamn it, her name's Margaret'

3 'It wasn't really her. It was a woman named Kay Francis. She's a white movie star who looks just like Mother Dear'

4 'Times are hard and friends are few / I take great pleasure in writing you / Will you be my Valentine?'

Identify the person(s) 'to whom' this comment refers.

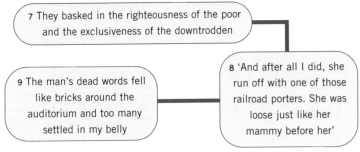

7 They basked in the righteousness of the poor and the exclusiveness of the downtrodden

9 The man's dead words fell like bricks around the auditorium and too many settled in my belly

8 'And after all I did, she run off with one of those railroad porters. She was loose just like her mammy before her'

Check your answers on page 88.

B *Consider these issues.*

a The importance of books to Maya and the influence Mrs Flowers has on her and her reading.

b What you learn from the incidences of white prejudice against Blacks.

c The extent to which Bailey is affected by the separation from his mother.

d Momma's method of dealing with Dr Lincoln's prejudice.

e What you have learned about the black community in Stamps.

f The continuing effect on Maya of the trauma of rape.

CHAPTER 25

Bailey is shocked by the hatred of the Whites

Momma tells the children that she is taking them to their parents in California. Maya suspects the reason for this move is concern for Bailey. A few weeks previously he had witnessed a black man being pulled out of the pond, and had been made to help carry the body. Bailey had been shocked by the obvious hatred and contempt in the eyes and voices of the white men who were there.

Due to financial difficulties, it is decided that Momma will take Maya first and that Bailey can follow a month later. Maya grieves for this temporary loss of Bailey, for Uncle Willie, who had never previously been separated from his mother, and for Louise, her first friend.

COMMENT   Bailey's experience makes clear the brutality of life in the South and reinforces the image of racial hatred established in the previous chapter.

It is implied that Momma has decided to move the children because of their growing awareness of the surrounding racial hatred.

GLOSSARY   **D'Artagnan** a character created by Alexandre Dumas (1802–70), a French writer who had one white and one black parent and whose grandmother was a slave
the Count of Monte Cristo a character in the book, *The Count of Monte Cristo*, written by Alexandre Dumas
The Fall of the House of Usher a 'grotesque' short story by Edgar Allan Poe, written in 1839
Didn't Moses … deliver Daniel? biblical references (in these cases the enslaved nation of Israel) which indicate that the downtrodden will receive justice eventually
djinn variation of jinnee, meaning an intelligent spirit which has power over people, and can appear in human and animal forms

CHAPTER 26

Maya recognises the deep emotion that underpins the meeting between Momma and her mother. She and Momma settle in Los Angeles (see Map of States on p. 8) while her mother returns to San Francisco to make arrangements. Bailey arrives a month later and over the next six months they are occasionally visited by their father. It is many years after that Maya is able to reflect with pride on how Momma successfully adjusted to a totally alien environment. She is distressed to learn that when they leave for San Francisco Momma is to return to Arkansas (see Map on p. 8).

What are your impressions of Maya's mother?

They spend the first few months in a dingy apartment in Oakland and Maya becomes aware that the family is now less prosperous. She recalls affectionately when her mother awakened her and Bailey in the middle of the night to give them a party at which she sang and danced for them. Their mother works in bars playing pinochle (see Glossary) for money or running a poker game, proud that she is not a servant and uses her brains to earn a living. Her toughness, refusal to compromise and strength of temper are clearly displayed when she shoots her partner for calling her a 'bitch' (p. 202). The partner survives and they still hold each other in mutual respect.

After the start of the Second World War Maya's mother marries Daddy Clidell, who she describes as the first father she would know, and they move to San Francisco.

COMMENT   Momma's remarkable strength of character and inner resourcefulness is demonstrated in her ability to adjust to life in Los Angeles.

Maya's mother is portrayed as a vibrant, exciting and potentially dangerous woman.

GLOSSARY   **Lucky Strike** a brand of cigarette

pinochle a trick-taking card game which uses two packs and where all cards below nines are left out, can be played with large groups of people

CHAPTER 27

Maya feels at home in San Francisco   At the beginning of the Second World War many Japanese left San Francisco's Fillmore district to be replaced by Negroes moving up from the South, who welcomed the opportunity of work and showed no sympathy for the exiled Japanese. In these times of confusion, fear and change Maya starts to feel more at home and grows to love the city, although she always remains aware of the presence of racism bred from a history of ignorance, distrust and fear. She recalls one story of a white woman who refused to sit next to a black man on a bus, accusing him of being a 'draft dodger' (p. 208), only to discover he had lost his arm while fighting for his country.

COMMENT   Maya supposes the black population did not sympathise with the Japanese partly because they were gaining so much. Additionally, as the Japanese were not white and therefore not to be feared, there was no need to consider their plight.

Maya's identification with her new home has much to do with her constant sense that life is a risky business.

GLOSSARY   **Axis agent** an agent for the alliance of Germany, Italy and Japan in the Second World War

draft dodger a person who avoids being conscripted into the army

Iwo Jima an island in the West Pacific and the scene of prolonged fighting between US and Japanese forces

CHAPTER 28

Maya does well at school

Maya does not settle in her local high school and is transferred to George Washington High School which lies outside the black neighbourhood and is attended, predominantly, by white students. She is inspired by the teaching of Miss Kirwin and, because of her, starts to read the newspapers and high quality magazines. She gains confidence through being accepted as the equal of the white students. At fourteen Maya is awarded a scholarship to the California Labor School, taking drama and dance as additional options.

COMMENT   The acceptance of Maya by her teacher, with no favouritism and no prejudice, leads to her intellectual growth and to her increased self-esteem.

Note Maya's 'allegiances' at this stage in the novel: 'Momma with her solemn determination, Mrs Flowers and her books, Bailey with his love, my mother and her gaiety, Miss Kirwin and her information, my evening classes of drama and dance' (p. 212).

CALIFORNIA

GLOSSARY pompadours type of hat

       Basil Rathbone an English actor, well known for his portrayal of
       Sherlock Holmes

       Bette Davis a famous film star

CHAPTER *29*

Maya's house is filled with a succession of tenants. Her admiration for her stepfather, Daddy Clidell, grows as she realises he is a man of strength, tenderness and fairness who, with little education, has become successful. Maya benefits from these qualities and also from his expert knowledge of cards. She is introduced to his friends who entertain her with their stories. She recalls in particular a scam in which con men Mr Red Leg and his friend Just Black cheated a white man, well *Do you think the* known for his hatred of Negroes, of forty thousand *white man was* dollars. Whilst recognising the illegality of the fraud, *treated unfairly?* Maya takes pride in the achievements of these men who have used their skills to gain a victory.

She comments on the difference between her formal and informal education in language. In school she is taught in the same way as the Whites, but on the streets she learns the colloquial language of the Blacks.

COMMENT Maya shows her admiration for those who use the skills they have to make something of themselves in a world that is generally not on their side.

GLOSSARY roomers lodgers

       tonk and high, low, Jick, Jack and the Game types of card games

       C.C.C. Civilian Conservation Corps, founded in 1933

       Lucullan feast Lucullus was a successful Roman general whose
       days of retirement were spent in a life of luxury

A Identify the speaker.

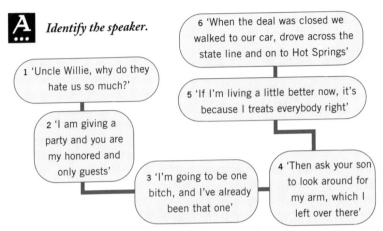

6 'When the deal was closed we walked to our car, drove across the state line and on to Hot Springs'

1 'Uncle Willie, why do they hate us so much?'

5 'If I'm living a little better now, it's because I treats everybody right'

2 'I am giving a party and you are my honored and only guests'

3 'I'm going to be one bitch, and I've already been that one'

4 'Then ask your son to look around for my arm, which I left over there'

Identify the person(s) 'to whom' this comment refers.

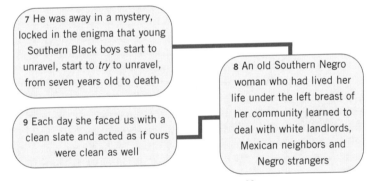

7 He was away in a mystery, locked in the enigma that young Southern Black boys start to unravel, start to *try* to unravel, from seven years old to death

8 An old Southern Negro woman who had lived her life under the left breast of her community learned to deal with white landlords, Mexican neighbors and Negro strangers

9 Each day she faced us with a clean slate and acted as if ours were clean as well

Check your answers on page 88.

B Consider these issues.

a Why Momma decides to take the children back to California.

b The plight of the Japanese at the start of the Second World War.

c Evidence of racism in San Francisco.

d The importance of Miss Kirwin to Maya's development.

e How both Mother and the children benefited from the presence of Daddy Clidell.

f Why Maya takes such delight in the triumphs of the black storytellers.

Father and mother

Chapter 30

Maya is invited to spend the summer with her father in southern California. She is shocked that Dolores, his father's girlfriend, is so young, whilst Dolores had been expecting a child of eight instead of a six-foot tall, fifteen-year-old. Maya is disappointed to find her father lives in a trailer park outside town and is unimpressed by Dolores's efforts at homemaking. Increasingly she and Dolores come into conflict, much to her father's obvious amusement.

Maya sees a different side to her father

Maya's father, an excellent cook, travels weekly to Mexico (see Map of States on p. 8), supposedly to buy ingredients. On one occasion Maya is delighted to learn she is to accompany him. Dolores's silent response suggests she is not impressed. Maya enjoys the adventure of the journey, noticing closely how her father appears to be on good terms with the border guard. Instead of going to Ensenada, as she had expected, they stop at a *cantina* where her father is warmly greeted. Maya is treated kindly and her formal Spanish is received with delight. She sees a new side to her father, who is clearly a frequent visitor, and realises that he is a lonely person who had never belonged in Stamps, nor in the many places he had been since. Here he seems at home, admired and liked by both men and women simply for who he is.

As the day progresses the party atmosphere increases and Maya happily joins in the dancing. Later in the evening, when she cannot find her father, she begins to panic, convinced he has abandoned her. When she sees his car she realises he is with a woman and relishes the pain this would cause Dolores. But she soon becomes fearful and wonders how her father could leave her in this situation. Eventually he returns, clearly drunk, and, despite never having driven a car, Maya decides to drive home. The hazardous, exhilarating journey ends with

Maya crashing at the border. Chaos ensues until eventually her father is woken and, handling the situation with great skill, he enables them to resume their journey. The earlier happiness and joy of the day is lost as they drive home in silence.

COMMENT   Maya starts to understand her father and to acknowledge the difficulties he has in settling in any one place.

Maya's father behaves irresponsibly towards his daughter and appears to lack any sensitivity towards her needs.

The drive back from the *cantina* gives Maya a tremendous sense of power and control and shows real daring and determination.

GLOSSARY   **Jane Withers and Donald O'Connor** filmstars
Frigidaire a type of fridge
seersucker material with a puckered surface
mercados stores that sell exotic food
adobe huts huts made of mud
Tyrone Power ... Katina Paxinou more film stars
bronco-busting rodeo a horse event where the riders pit
   themselves against the wildness of the horses
St. Vitus Dance an involuntary jerkiness in the knees
Borracho drunk; a Spanish word. Note that the meanings of
   these words can be found in any English – Spanish dictionary

CHAPTER 31

Dolores wounds Maya

On their return an argument quickly develops between her father and Dolores, who accuses him of letting his children come between them. He reveals that he agrees with Maya's comment that she is 'a pretentious little bitch' (p. 237) and then leaves, slamming the door behind him. Maya, believing her father has treated his girlfriend unfairly, tries to appease her. Dolores, however, accuses her of eavesdropping and calls her mother 'a whore' (p. 239). They start to fight. Maya is stabbed and takes refuge in her father's car, still pursued by a furious Dolores. Her father appears, takes Dolores into the house, and returns to find his daughter bleeding. He takes her to a friend who treats her kindly and bandages the wound, saving her father the embarrassment of the incident being made public. That night she sleeps in the trailer of other friends of her father's.

The following morning her father visits her, gives her a dollar and a half and promises to return later. With only a few sandwiches and three dollars and some Mexican coins to her name, Maya decides to leave. She resolves not to return to her mother, knowing she would see the wound in her side and because she is still haunted by the guilt associated with Mr Freeman.

COMMENT

Her father's treatment of Dolores makes Maya see his unfairness and therefore causes Maya to overcome her own feelings of dislike in a genuine attempt to comfort Dolores.

Maya's father again behaves irresponsibly, leaving his injured daughter with friends and taking almost a perverse delight in the arguing between her and Dolores.

With her father's apparent abandonment of her, Maya's lack of self-confidence and feelings of guilt surface.

GLOSSARY   **banshee** a released female spirit, making a lot of noise

                         a Mason, an Elk men's clubs of a somewhat secretive nature

CHAPTER 32

In what ways do the homeless children support each other?

Maya wanders aimlessly until she finds a junkyard and she sleeps in an old car. When she wakes up she is surrounded by the faces of black, Mexican and white children who all sleep rough. She is welcomed and, in the month she spends there, she learns to drive, comes second in a dancing competition and spends her free time looking for and selling old bottles. Strongly impressed by the acceptance and lack of criticism in this strange and new society, she learns a tolerance that is to remain with her through life. After a month she telephones her mother who sends her the fare for the journey home. On her arrival, her mother decides that her father has not been feeding her enough.

COMMENT

This experience has a lasting effect on Maya. She has experienced people of different races working together, without prejudice, for the common good.

When Maya returns home it is perhaps typical of her that she does not reveal where she has been. Her mother's lack of curiosity suggests her father has said nothing about her disappearance.

GLOSSARY   **Brobdingnag** a place in Jonathan Swift's *Gulliver's Travels*, where the inhabitants are extremely tall

CHAPTER 33

Bailey leaves home

On Maya's return she immediately notices a difference in Bailey who, at sixteen, now seems much older and more distant. They communicate best when dancing and go regularly to the city auditorium.

There are problems between Bailey and his mother and some of the close ties between them need to be loosened. One night Bailey does not come home until one o'clock, despite having to be in by eleven. At his mother's anger he announces that he is leaving straight away and Maya watches helplessly as he packs his things and goes.

In the morning her mother's eyes are red. Maya, guessing where Bailey has gone, decides to visit him. He too has been crying but Maya is surprised to learn that her mother has already been there to talk things over and is to arrange a job for him with a friend in Oakland. Bailey says he sees his move as the inevitable consequence of growing up and is optimistic about his future. Maya is unable to find the words to express herself and leaves, offering him whatever support she can give.

COMMENT   Both Bailey and his mother seem to come to the realisation that their strong attachment needs to be loosened if he is to move into the adult world.

Maya's unease at parting from Bailey is, in part, due to her inability to articulate her thoughts and feelings at the time.

GLOSSARY   zoot suits smart suits with a long, loose jacket and high-waisted, tapered trousers
Oedipal skein a classical term describing the complex relationship between a mother and son
Switzerland in World War II a country which remained neutral in the Second World War

CHAPTER 34

What qualities does Maya show in her search for work?

At fifteen, Maya decides she wants to work as a conductor on the San Francisco streetcars, despite her mother's warning that Blacks are not accepted. For three weeks she persists and, finding her way blocked at every turning, she starts to feel alienated from the city she had grown to love. Throughout this period she is supported wholeheartedly by her mother who perceives the importance of the struggle. Finally, after numerous tests and falsified application forms, she becomes the 'first Negro on the San Francisco streetcars' (p. 262).

As she struggles to meet the demands of repeatedly difficult shift work, which she suspects is her punishment for having been awarded the job, her mother's continued support is invaluable.

By spring Maya decides to return to school but finds herself out of step with her peers. Her experiences of life have set her apart and the lessons at school seem irrelevant and tedious. She starts to play truant but stops when her mother gives her the choice not to go to school. She reflects on the teenage years as being hazardous ones where many surrender to adult expectations of conformity. These times are even more difficult, she believes, for black girls, and argues that those who struggle and retain and gain integrity and strength should be respected for their achievement.

COMMENT   The ingrained prejudice which Maya comes across in her determined attempt to work on the streetcars, and the lack of support from the black organisations, demonstrates the difficulties faced by all young, ambitious Blacks.

This episode demonstrates the strength of Maya's mother and the wisdom of her advice, encapsulated in her use of aphorisms (see Literary Terms).

Always a loner, Maya now feels increasingly isolated from her contemporaries as she searches for a different kind of life.

GLOSSARY   streetcars San Francisco trams
Guam an island in the North Pacific

CHAPTER 35

Maya becomes aware of lesbianism and begins to question her own sexuality. She questions her mother about the changes in her body and is hugely relieved by her direct and reassuring answers. A few weeks later, however, Maya finds herself moved by the sight of her friend's breasts and her anxiety returns. In an attempt to resolve the question of her sexuality she plans to seduce one of the handsome brothers who lived on her street. As the chosen brother walks past her, she bluntly invites him to have 'a sexual intercourse' (p. 274) with her. He readily agrees, his vanity, according to Maya, blinding him of the possibility that she was taking from him rather than giving. They go to a room of one of his friends and have sex in a markedly unromantic and clumsy fashion. Maya does not enjoy the experience, which does not have a great impact on her, and she remains confused. Three weeks later she finds she is pregnant.

COMMENT   Maya's concerns about her sexuality are those of a normal teenager. Her solution, however, is more than a little drastic and suggests great confusion and insecurity.

GLOSSARY   Richard Arlen ... Veronica Lake both are film stars
jolly sissies term of mild abuse, referring to men who may appear to be transsexual
hermaphrodite having both male and female sexual organs

CHAPTER 36

Maya's son is born   The only comfort Maya can take from her pregnancy is that, for her, it proves she cannot be lesbian. She realises her predicament is of her own making and writes to Bailey, who is at sea and advises her not to tell their mother and to continue to work for her high school diploma. She hides her pregnancy and actually begins to find school and learning exciting again. When Maya is six months pregnant her mother leaves for Alaska, still unaware of her daughter's condition. Only after she receives her high school diploma does Maya tell her stepfather Daddy Clidell that she is pregnant. Both he and her mother are astonished that she is to have the baby in three weeks' time. There is no pressure put on her to involve the father of the child and her stepfather ensures that she is well cared for. When her son is born she feels he is totally hers yet is afraid to touch him and dreads the possibility of damaging him. When he is three weeks old Maya's mother places him in bed with Maya and insists he stays there. Despite her fears she falls asleep and is woken by her mother to find him sleeping, safely sheltered by her arm.

COMMENT   Maya's mother and stepfather's sensible and positive response to her pregnancy help her to accept the responsibility of motherhood.

Despite the many traumas of Maya's young life the book ends on a very positive note. The final image is one of comfort, tenderness and security, offering optimism and hope for the future.

GLOSSARY   **brouhaha** fuss
V-Day victory days which celebrate the end of the Second World War
bassinet wickerwork or wooden cradle

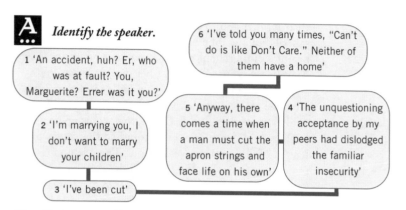

A Identify the speaker.

1 'An accident, huh? Er, who was at fault? You, Marguerite? Errer was it you?'

6 'I've told you many times, "Can't do is like Don't Care." Neither of them have a home'

2 'I'm marrying you, I don't want to marry your children'

5 'Anyway, there comes a time when a man must cut the apron strings and face life on his own'

4 'The unquestioning acceptance by my peers had dislodged the familiar insecurity'

3 'I've been cut'

Identify the person(s) 'to whom' this comment refers.

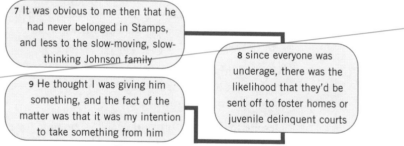

7 It was obvious to me then that he had never belonged in Stamps, and less to the slow-moving, slow-thinking Johnson family

8 since everyone was underage, there was the likelihood that they'd be sent off to foster homes or juvenile delinquent courts

9 He thought I was giving him something, and the fact of the matter was that it was my intention to take something from him

Check your answers on page 88.

B Consider these issues.

a What you have learned about Maya's father and his capabilities as a parent.

b The reasons for the absence of prejudice amongst the children living in the junkyard.

c Why Maya is finally successful in her efforts to work on the streetcars.

d The different images shown of Maya's mother and her capabilities as a parent.

e How Maya's sexual insecurities, stemming back to being raped at the age of eight, are reflected in her behaviour as a teenager.

f The extent to which the novel ends on a positive note and why the writer chose to do so.

PART THREE

COMMENTARY

THEMES

This is not a novel that lends itself easily to a clear definition of themes, partly because of its **autobiographical** aspects and its **episodic** (see Literary Terms) nature. There are, however, certain ideas that are explored and connections that are made in the course of the story.

FAMILY

Maya and her brother Bailey have no stable family life and yet family is very important to both of them. As a result of the break-up of their parents' marriage, when Maya is three and Bailey four, they are sent to Stamps, Arkansas (see Map of States on p. 8) to be raised by their paternal grandmother and their Uncle Willie. They soon settle in their new home and grow accustomed to the ways of their grandmother ('Momma') and uncle. They are raised in a strict, God-fearing fashion, combined with love and a strong sense of security. This is, nevertheless, disturbed by thoughts of being unwanted by their natural parents, from time to time. One Christmas, when they receive presents from their parents, their main response is to wonder what they had done that was so wrong that they should be sent away.

At seven, when Maya's father arrives, her world is thrown into confusion and she is understandably frightened by the thought of returning to California with him. The move introduces the children to a new and very different area of family life. Grandmother and Grandfather Baxter, their mother's parents, have a very strong sense of family which is inherited by their

mother and her five brothers. It is said of the brothers
that they have no need of friends, as they have each
other. When Maya's mother is insulted at work her
brothers attack the offender, leaving him close to death.
When Maya is raped by Mr Freeman he is killed whilst
on bail and it is implied that the brothers were also
responsible for this.

Maya's mother and father are central figures in her life,
both in their absence and their presence. As parents,
their inadequacies are made clear. They have little
contact with their children throughout the early years in
Stamps and when they first appear in the story they are
glamorous but distant figures, bringing fun but not
stability into the children's lives. The father remains
distant and a stranger, though Maya is not condemning
in her appraisal of him. On the trip to Mexico she
recognises his inability to find a place for himself in the
world and shows understanding of his true nature: 'It
seemed hard to believe that he was a lonely person,
searching relentlessly in bottles, under women's skirts,
in church work and lofty job titles for his "personal
niche", lost before birth and unrecovered since' (p. 226,
Chapter 30).

Maya's mother plays a more substantial role in her life,
particularly in her teenage years. She supports her
daughter in her efforts to work on the streetcars, deals
with her truancy and sexual insecurities in a sensible
way and is not condemning when Maya reveals she is
pregnant. Perhaps, ironically, it is her mother who is by
her side at the end of the story when helping her to
come to terms with the responsibility of parenthood.

EDUCATION AND LEARNING

Both Maya and Bailey are academically able children.
They do well at school and love reading. As a young

child Maya reads widely across the works of both
English and American writers, but it is Shakespeare
who is her 'first white love' (p. 14, Chapter 2). In St
Louis (see Map on p. 8) she joins a library and spends
most of her Saturdays there losing herself in the world
of fiction. Her reading tastes are wide and she also
enjoys the comic strips and reads them avidly. She is
encouraged in her interest by Mrs Flowers (see Chapter
15) and, later, by Miss Kirwin (see Chapter 28), women
for whom she has enormous respect and admiration.
Throughout the novel reading is portrayed both as a
means of escape and as a way of broadening one's mind
and one's horizons, and it is full of literary references.

Maya graduates while still living in Stamps. This is an
important occasion for the family and for the black
community, who celebrate educational success with
presents and a ceremony. The unfairness of the
educational system, where Whites and Blacks are
segregated, is, however, made clear in the speech of Mr
Donleavy. He speaks of the wonderful resources being
given to the school which the Whites attend, and
highlights the limited expectations of black children in
comparison.

When Maya attends the George Washington High
School in San Francisco, where she is one of only three
black students, she feels she is finally at a 'real school'
(p. 209, Chapter 28). There, she meets students more
able than herself and is inspired by the teaching of Miss
Kirwin who 'never seemed to notice that I was Black
and therefore different' (p. 211, Chapter 28). At
fourteen she is given a scholarship to attend the
California Labor School where she studies drama and
dance. After leaving school temporarily to work on the
streetcars, she returns to find it holds little interest for
her. She starts to play truant but stops when her mother
wisely gives her the freedom to attend school or not. It

is pregnancy that gives school back its magic as Maya tries to bury herself in her work, successfully achieving her diploma only three weeks before her baby is born.

BLACK AND WHITE

As a child Maya has difficulty coming to terms with her blackness and believes she will one day emerge with white hair and blue eyes. Through the course of the story she explores what being black means to a young girl growing up in the southern state of Arkansas. She sees evidence of unfairness all around her: in the disrespectful treatment of her grandmother and uncle by young white children, in the inequalities of the education system, in the terror evoked by the Ku Klux Klan (see Glossary in Chapter 3, Detailed Summaries) and in the sheer harshness of her neighbours' lives. Even in the more tolerant San Francisco she is aware of racism as a pervasive force in everyday life and has to fight for the right to work on the streetcars.

Whites are, for the most part, not portrayed sympathetically in this story. Their sense of superiority is made clear through characters such as the ex-sheriff, who comes to warn the family about the Klan; Mrs Cullinan, who changes her servants' names for convenience; Mr Donleavy, who so nearly ruins the graduation ceremony; and Dr Lincoln, who refuses to treat Maya because she is black. The sheer hatred and contempt of some white people is forcefully experienced by Bailey when a black man's body is pulled from the pond.

The Whites, generally, have a better standard of living and Maya is astonished by their wastefulness, yet impressed by their possessions. She delights always in 'Negroes' who, one way or another, rise above the poverty and restrictions of their situation to triumph over the Whites. Thus she is delighted by Henry Reed's valedictory *coup*, by Joe Louis's victory, by Mr Red Leg's scam and by her own success on the streetcars. On an equal level she is dismayed to see her fellows accepting unfair treatment and failing to fight back. She is angered by the cotton pickers' meek acceptance of their miserable work conditions, by the graduation audience's silent reception of Mr Donleavy's speech and by Momma's failure to question the beliefs with which she had been raised.

It is not until she enters the world of the homeless children in the junkyard that Maya experiences an environment free from racial prejudice and distrust. For the first time she feels herself to be part of a 'brotherhood of man' (p. 247, Chapter 32) and comes to appreciate the virtues of acceptance and tolerance and to incorporate them into her own life.

DISPLACEMENT

At the end of the prologue, Maya Angelou writes 'If growing up is painful for the Southern Black girl, being aware of her displacement is the rust on the razor that threatens the throat' (p. 6). What she means by displacement depends upon the interpretation of the reader. Certainly it has at least two levels of meaning relevant to *I Know Why the Caged Bird Sings*.

Maya and Bailey were moved from their home in California to the very different environment of Stamps. Later they were to live in St Louis, Los Angeles and San Francisco. They were secure in Stamps and accepted by the community, but only as 'a real mother embraces a stranger's child' (p. 7, Chapter 1) and, after their stay in St Louis they were regarded as 'the travelers' (p. 87, Chapter 14). In St Louis they were set apart from their peers by their superior education,

and when they have to move house again Maya simply
sees this as a sign that their lives were destined to 'be
different from everyone else's in the world' (p. 67,
Chapter 10).

Throughout the story we are made aware of the writer's
need for a sense of permanence and a reluctance to
become too attached to any one place generated by this
lack of stability in her life. For much of their childhood
Maya and Bailey felt they were responsible for their
parents' abandonment of them and when they are
reunited the fear that their parents may, once again,
disappear is always present. It is not until Maya lives in
San Francisco that she finds a home with which she can
identify and feel a part of. Ironically it is the very 'air of
collective displacement' and 'the impermanence of life
in wartime' (p. 205, Chapter 27) that makes Maya feel
so at ease. She seems to thrive on change and seems
spurred on to do so, sometimes for no apparent reason,
for instance when she decides to leave school and go to
work: 'the need for change bulldozed a road down the
center of my mind' (p. 257, Chapter 34).

The inability to settle in one place is a quality which
Maya comes to recognise in her father. In Mexico she
acknowledges his loneliness and his constant search for
acceptance and recognition. Her comment that his
place in the world was 'lost before birth and
unrecovered since' (p. 226, Chapter 30) encourages the
reader to think of other types of displacement. In the
broader sense we see a whole race of people who have
been displaced. Through slavery, the Blacks were
transported from their homeland of Africa to a foreign
country where they were abused and subjected to gross
intolerance and prejudice. It is in this foreign country
that the descendants of those earlier slaves must find
their way and make their home. Some, like Maya's
father, are never able to do so. Others, like her

grandmother, with her apparently effortless acceptance
of life in Los Angeles, seem to have an endless capacity
to adapt and change. Is it any wonder then that she
argues that the emergence of the 'formidable' American
Negro female is the 'outcome of the struggle won by
survivors' (p. 265, Chapter 34)?

STRUCTURE

The story traces the writer's life from the age of three
through her childhood and early teenage years (see
bildungsroman in Literary Terms). It is roughly in
chronological order (see Literary Terms), though it is
not always possible to tell when particular events take
place. We do not, for instance, know how old Maya is
in the opening incident in the Colored Methodist
Episcopal Church in the Preface. The story is **episodic**
(see Literary Terms) in its nature, with some chapters
covering a range of varied events and others focusing on
single significant episodes. Thus in Chapter 4 we read
about Mr McElroy, the importance of Bailey to Maya,
the custom of preserving food in Stamps, Maya's
journey into the white part of town and her confusion
about Whites in general. In contrast Chapter 5 is
devoted entirely to describing the white girls' attempts
to humiliate Momma.

Some of the characters, such as Mr McElroy, and many
of the incidents described stand independent of the
storyline as a whole, with little reference backwards or
forwards. Cumulatively, however, they portray the
growth of the writer, physically, emotionally and
intellectually.

It is place that probably gives the story its most obvious
structural feature. Starting in Stamps, then moving to
St Louis, back to Stamps, then on to Los Angeles

and San Francisco, the writer groups her memories around the particular place and the people who lived there. Each place has its own distinctive characteristics, whether it be the emphasis on community in Stamps and the routine and homeliness of life in the Store, or on family in St Louis, or on the physical environment in San Francisco. Sometimes events are recounted simply with little authorial comment. Others are used to make a point or develop a particular line of thought. In Chapter 31 when Maya writes about how Dolores injured her and her father all but deserted her, the events are allowed to speak for themselves. In Chapter 34, however, the motives of the receptionist of the Market Street Railway Company are analysed and explained in some detail.

At the heart of the structure of the novel lies the traumatic rape of Maya when she was eight years old. The preceding chapters help you to understand Maya as a young child and to appreciate the insecurity and longing for affection which lead her to act as she did. Everything following the rape is inevitably coloured by the effect it had on her life and her perceptions of the people and events around her. There is, by the end of the story, some sense of resolution and settlement of internal conflict as Maya sleeps, her arm protectively guarding her new-born son. However, as this is the first of several autobiographies, there is also the sense that this story only contains the early chapters of her life and that there is more to follow.

MAYA

The narrator and the main character, Maya Angelou is at the heart of the story. You see events through her eyes, recollected from childhood memory, with an adult view, at times, imposed on them.

She is a solitary child, relying heavily on her brother Bailey for comfort and companionship. Although there is an underlying sense of insecurity during her first five-year stay in Stamps, it is not an unhappy time for her and she finds comfort in the routines of the Store and family life. She is a conscientious child, doing her chores carefully and punishing herself if she makes a mistake. She is also observant and sensitive to what is going on around her. When Uncle Willie pretends not to be disabled she empathises with him, understanding, in part, the reasons for his actions. When she sees Momma standing firm against the insults of the white girls she senses rather than understands her victory and responds by raking hearts in the dust.

The narrator
Insecure
Sensitive
Intelligent
Determined
Hates injustice

Watchful and always wary, Maya is hesitant when confronted with change. When her father arrives she is proud of him but constantly threatened by the thought that he will soon go. When he does eventually leave the children in St Louis she feels nothing, regarding him as a stranger. Her response to her mother is similar. She admires her and is proud of her, but it is only in the closing chapters of the book that you begin to sense an emotional closeness. It is her need for emotional and physical warmth that drives her to respond to Mr Freeman. Her innocence is painfully evident in her desire to be held by him and to feel safe in the 'encasement in his big arms' (p. 73, Chapter 11). It is not only her body that is violated at the age of eight but also her trust. She feels guilty for what has happened, is unable to tell the truth in the courtroom and accepts responsibility for Mr Freeman's death. The experience drives her to silence and it is a year before she finds her 'first life line' (p. 90, Chapter 15) in the form of Mrs Flowers.

As a child, Maya is clearly academically bright. She does well at school and reads extensively in her free time. It is this love of reading that forms the basis of her relationship with Mrs Flowers who lends her books and encourages her to read aloud. Feeling respected and liked for who she is Maya gradually starts the long road to recovery. At eleven she makes her first friend Louise who, like herself, is 'a lonely girl' (p. 136, Chapter 20) and shortly afterwards she finds herself sought after by Tommy Valdon. Both experiences help to build her confidence, as do her subsequent academic successes in Stamps and in San Francisco (see Map on p. 8) where she thrives under the guidance of Miss Kirwin.

Whilst Maya's confidence may be low, she is never without spirit and the desire to fight against unfairness and injustice. When she is ten years old she rebels against Mrs Cullinan's attempt to call her 'Mary' for convenience. A few years later she pursues a job on the San Francisco streetcars with determination and becomes the first Black to work on them. She rejoices in the successes of Blacks, fully aware of the importance of Joe Louis's victory and proud of Mr Red Leg's ability to cheat a white man out of forty thousand dollars. It is in incidents such as these that we see most clearly the foundations of the woman who was, later in life, to become so involved in the Civil Rights Movement.

Maya, the child and young woman, is deeply confused and insecure yet, at the same time she shows courage, determination and a willingness to learn, to laugh and to take control of her own life. The opening of the story with its meaningful line 'I didn't come to stay' (p. 3) demonstrates her sense of displacement (see Theme on p. 63) which remains with her for much of her early life. Separated from her parents at the age of three her youth is spent moving from one place to another, never feeling a sense of permanence or belonging until finally she starts to identify with, and feel at home in, San Francisco. Ironically it is the 'undertone of fear' (p. 206) in the war-time city that contributes most to her 'sense of belonging' (p. 206, Chapter 27). By the end of the story, however, the heavy sense of impermanence is lifted. Though Maya's son is unplanned and the consequence perhaps of her lack of self-confidence, the story ends on a very positive note. You see Maya, the young mother, sheltering her three-week-old son as they lie sleeping. She has conquered her fears of hurting him, fears founded in her own awful childhood experiences, and the tone of the conclusion is one of comfort and hope, creating a sense of belonging as though the ghosts of the past have been laid to rest.

MOMMA

Maya's grandmother is a crucial figure in her childhood. She is a strong and determined woman, who has built up her business from a mobile lunch counter to a profitable store. A deeply religious woman, she lives by the commandments and provides a strict but very secure home for Maya and Bailey. Without being openly affectionate she cares for them deeply and they learn to rely on her love.

Whilst she believes it is best to keep away from whitefolk she is, nevertheless, prepared to fight for her rights and to preserve her dignity when she comes into contact with them. When the white girls insult her outside the Store she maintains a dignified stillness and emerges the victor. When Maya is rejected for dental treatment by Doctor Lincoln, Momma demands

Paternal
grandmother
Strong,
determined
Religious
Strict
Dignified

interest payment on the loan she gave him, sufficient to pay for the treatment elsewhere.

Devoted to Uncle Willie, her family and home, she is nevertheless prepared to leave it for several months to take the children to Los Angeles (see Map of States on p. 8) and, once there, she showed the capacity to adjust wholly to 'that foreign life' (p. 197, Chapter 26). For Maya she represents both power and strength and her 'deep-brooding love' (p. 55, Chapter 9) is a powerful force in the young girl's life.

BAILEY

Attractive
Lively
Insecure
Sensitive
Caring

Maya's older brother Bailey is probably the most important influence in her childhood and teenage years. At the age of four he shares her loss of parents and security and moves to Stamps to live with their grandmother. Maya looks up to him, admiring his physical attractiveness, his boldness and his vitality. He shares her love of Shakespeare, her sense of fun and laughter and her unhappiness at the loss of their parents. When they receive presents from their parents at Christmas Bailey cries. Also insecure, like Maya, he wonders if he is to blame for the loss of their parents. Unlike her, he adapts to the changes in his life more readily. He is keen to accompany his father to California and when he meets his mother he falls in love with her instantly and he cries when he is sent back to Stamps.

His sensitivity is shown in many ways. When Maya is raped she says nothing of it, for fear that Mr Freeman would kill Bailey. When he finally learns the truth his feelings for his sister are clearly demonstrated by the tears he sheds for her. He is deeply upset when he watches the film starring a woman who looks like his mother, so much so that he risks his life on the railway line. When the black man's body is pulled from the pond he is visibly shaken by the hostility and hatred of the white onlookers and searches to find a reason for it.

At sixteen Bailey breaks the ties with his mother and leaves home, offering Maya the chance to go with him and promising to take care of her. Later he gets a job at sea and, although Maya follows his advice when she is pregnant, you sense that the closeness of the early years has diminished with time and distance.

MOTHER

Glamorous
Beautiful
Exciting
Tough
Independent
Understanding

For much of the story Maya's mother is portrayed as a rather distant, glamorous and exciting person. When Maya first sees her mother she is struck by her beauty, believing this to be the reason she and Bailey had been sent away. She is tough, 'unflinchingly honest' (p. 200, Chapter 26) and able to stand up for herself. On one occasion she beats Pat Patterson almost to death for cursing her and on another she shoots her business partner for calling her a 'bitch' (Chapter 26). She works in bars and takes pride in her independence, being scornful of those who are in service. Whilst she has the power to hypnotise men she does not seem happy with her choice of partners, getting divorced from Maya's father when the children are very young and setting up home with Mr Freeman who damaged her daughter. She is, however, more fortunate in her second husband Daddy Clidell.

Despite her glamorous lifestyle, she has a strong motherly side to her character. When Maya is sick after being raped she cares for her tenderly. Later, when they are living in Oakland, she delights the children by holding a surprise party for them one night and by dancing and singing for them. She seems to understand and empathise with both of her children. When Bailey leaves home she recognises his need to separate from her. Far from taking it personally she goes to offer him help the next day. She understands and supports Maya in her efforts to work on the streetcars and it is to her that Maya turns when she is confused about her sexuality. When Maya is pregnant her mother does not condemn, but stands by her and helps her to accept her new-born child.

FATHER

Handsome
Lonely
Irresponsible
A misfit

Maya's first impression of her father is that he is 'blindingly handsome' (p. 53, Chapter 9). She takes pride in his apparent wealth and correct speech. She is, nevertheless, wary of him and unable to cope with his gentle teasing of her, describing him as 'the first cynic' (p. 53, Chapter 9) she had ever met. When he leaves her and Bailey with their mother in St Louis he is still a stranger to her.

Maya gets to see another side of her father when she is older and he takes her to Mexico. As she watches him mixing with the Mexicans, and being accepted for what he is, she realises he is a lonely person who for most of his life has been searching for the unattainable. His inadequacies as a father are, nevertheless, made clear to the reader during this episode. He leaves Maya to her own devices in a room full of strangers, returning hours later and very drunk. When Maya is cut by his girlfriend Dolores he takes her to a friend rather than the hospital, so as to avoid the incident becoming public knowledge and shaming him. He then leaves her overnight with some other friends, visiting briefly the next morning. When Maya finally returns to her mother, having been sleeping rough for a month, it is clear that her father had never reported her missing. Given his careless and irresponsible approach to parenthood, it is not surprising that Maya should identify Daddy Clidell as 'the first father I would know' (p. 203, Chapter 26).

MINOR CHARACTERS

Uncle Willie
Proud
Sensitive
Caring

The children's disabled uncle was injured as a child and now lives with his mother, helping to run the Store in Stamps. He is a proud man who takes great care with his appearance. His sensitivity about his disability is shown clearly when, on one occasion, he goes to great lengths to hide his lameness from a couple of strangers visiting the Store. Maya 'felt closer to him at that moment than ever before or since' (p. 14, Chapter 2). He shares responsibility for the children, at times beating them if they misbehave, for instance when they become hysterical in church. Maya loves him 'in my fashion' (p. 89, Chapter 14) and is anxious that he should not think ill of her.

Grandmother
Baxter
Powerful
Forceful
Determined

An unusual woman, Grandmother Baxter is a powerful figure in the black community of St Louis. The precinct captain and the mother of 'six mean children' (p. 60, Chapter 10), she is well known amongst the criminal fraternity and has influence in the police department. Though Negro in origin, she is white-skinned and was raised by a German family in Illinois. After the trial and murder of Mr Freeman, she forbids the children to ever mention his name again.

The Baxter
Brothers

Maya's five uncles, her mother's brothers, are a formidable force. They are well known in St Louis for their explosive tempers and their meanness. They have a strong sense of family, protecting each other and looking only to each other for company and friendship. It is implied, though not stated, that they were responsible for the death of Mr Freeman.

Mr Freeman	Maya's mother's boyfriend is a southerner and is described by Maya as being a big and flabby man. He comes across as a quiet and fairly withdrawn man, who is devoted to Maya's mother. However, he sexually abuses Maya on two occasions before violently raping her at the age of eight. Found guilty by the court he is nevertheless released on the day of the trial, only to be kicked to death the same day. Maya, who lies in court, feels guilty about the death of this man despite the extensive damage he has done to her.
Reverend Howard Thomas	An elder of the church, Reverend Thomas visits Stamps every three months, staying with Momma whenever he does so. Both Maya and Bailey dislike him intensely, not just because he is obese and ugly, but because whenever he stays he ruins Sunday breakfast by praying for so long that the food goes cold. He also eats the best part of the chicken at dinner. The children take great delight in seeing him humiliated in church by Sister Monroe.
Louise Kendricks	Described as a pretty but lonely girl, Louise becomes Maya's first friend when they meet at the summer picnic. Maya identifies with her and admires her for being 'able to fall in the sky and admit it' (p. 137, Chapter 20). Their friendship flourishes and is an important boost to Maya's self-esteem.
Mrs Flowers	Mrs Flowers is a friend of Momma's and a source of inspiration to Maya who regards her as the 'aristocrat of Black Stamps' (p. 90, Chapter 15). It is she who draws Maya out of her self-made shell after she is raped and gives her the confidence of knowing she is liked for who she is. She achieves this by building on Maya's love of books and by encouraging her to read aloud.
Miss Kirwin	A white teacher at the George Washington High School, Miss Kirwin inspires Maya to read more widely. She treats all her students alike, showing no

discrimination between Black or White. Stimulating in her approach, Maya writes of her as being 'the only teacher I remembered' (p. 211, Chapter 28).

Mr McElroy   Maya is fascinated by this man who lives close to the Store, owning his own house and land. He is not a sociable man and does not go to church, though he maintains a friendly relationship with Momma. As a child Maya finds him mysterious and unique in his position of independence, though as an adult she sees him as a relatively simple and uninteresting man.

Mr Donleavy   Mr Donleavy is the white man who comes to talk at the graduation ceremony in Stamps. His speech is full of racist assumptions and innuendoes, which depress Maya and the rest of the audience.

Henry Reed   A fellow pupil of Maya's in Stamps and one she much admires. It is he who saves the graduation ceremony, following the speech of Mr Donleavy, by leading the audience and the students in the Negro National Anthem.

Sister Monroe   A resident of Stamps who delights the children by embarrassing Reverend Thomas at church on Sunday.

LANGUAGE & STYLE

The story is **autobiographical** in content and takes the form of a **first-person narrative** (see Literary Terms). By telling her story in this way Maya Angelou creates the sense that she is talking directly to her reader, revealing incidents and thoughts almost as they would be revealed in speech. She 'speaks' to the reader as if we know her, assuming the reader has the same knowledge of literature, history, culture and Americanisms as she does – and thus making the Glossaries in Part Two of these Notes very necessary.

Maya moves with ease between her childhood
experience and her adult views. When she describes the
lives of the cotton pickers in Chapter 1, for example,
she incorporates details of her adult rage at the
stereotyped picture of the 'song-singing cotton pickers'
(p. 10). Maya Angelou tries to explore and explain the
impressions and experiences of her past, at times
shifting the narrative into the present tense. When she
recalls her desire for a boyfriend she does so in the light
of her present beliefs: 'I believe most plain girls are
virtuous because of the scarcity of opportunity to be
otherwise' (p. 273, Chapter 35).

Her descriptive style varies. At times you find a wealth
of detail, as when she describes the food in St Louis
(pp. 60–1, Chapter 10) or the attractions of San
Francisco (pp. 206–7, Chapter 27). People are brought
to life by her attention to their actions as well as their
appearances. When describing Bailey in Chapter 4 she
shows him in conversation with the old ladies, stealing
pickles from the Store and at play with other children.
By portraying him in these different lights she brings
him to life for the reader.

• At other times the language is restrained, yet no less
powerful for being so. Maya describes Mr Freeman
after he has raped her, using a single effective **simile**
(see Literary Terms): 'He leaned over, his whole face a
threat that could have smothered me' (p. 78, Chapter
12). She uses the same technique when she writes about
her mother as being 'a hurricane in its perfect power'
(p. 58, Chapter 9). Of the rape itself she writes 'Then
there was the pain' (p. 76, Chapter 12), conveying
clearly, in those five simple words, the horror of the
experience.

Sometimes more stylised language is used for particular
effect. When writing about the Ku Klux Klan she twice
uses the rhetorical question 'Boys?' and proceeds to

define them as 'The ugliness and rottenness of old abominations' (p. 18, Chapter 3).

As a young child Maya was very aware of, and embarrassed by, Momma's dialect as contrasted with the more formal speech of Mrs Flowers (p. 92, Chapter 15). By her teenage years, however, she has learned to slip between the colloquial language of the street and the more standard form of the classroom, slipping between 'That's not unusual' and 'It be's like that sometimes' (p. 219, Chapter 29).

In writing direct speech Maya Angelou uses the dialect appropriate to her characters. Momma speaks in the colloquial style common to most residents of Stamps. Maya's father's speech is, however, more formal, possibly reflecting his time spent living in the North and, more likely, his wish to distance himself from the place of his birth. Interestingly, his speech is littered with 'er' and 'errer' (p. 53, Chapter 9), a characteristic which delights Maya and yet emphasises the perception of him as an indecisive and rather weak man.

Note that in contrast to the capitalisation used in York Notes where both 'Black' and 'White' are capitalised if nouns and not if adjectives, Maya Angelou always gives 'Black' a capital but does not with the word 'white'. Consider why the writer does this and what she hopes to achieve by doing so.

PART FOUR

Study skills

How to use quotations

One of the secrets of success in writing essays is the way you use quotations. There are five basic principles:
- Put inverted commas at the beginning and end of the quotation
- Write the quotation exactly as it appears in the original
- Do not use a quotation that repeats what you have just written
- Use the quotation so that it fits into your sentence
- Keep the quotation as short as possible

Quotations should be used to develop the line of thought in your essays.

Your comment should not duplicate what is in your quotation. For example:

> Maya tells us how important Bailey was to her by presenting him as her Kingdom Come, 'My pretty Black brother was my Kingdom Come'.

Far more effective is to write:

> The importance of Bailey in her life is clearly demonstrated when she writes, 'My pretty Black brother was my Kingdom Come'.

The most sophisticated way of using the writer's words is to embed them into your sentence:

> Bailey, Maya's 'pretty Black brother', played a central role in her life and was, as she describes, her 'Kingdom Come'.

When you use quotations in this way, you are demonstrating the ability to use text as evidence to support your ideas - not simply including words from the original to prove you have read it.

Everyone writes differently. Work through the suggestions given here and adapt the advice to suit your own style and interests. This will improve your essay-writing skills and allow your personal voice to emerge.

The following points indicate in ascending order the skills of essay writing:

- Picking out one or two facts about the story and adding the odd detail
- Writing about the text by retelling the story
- Retelling the story and adding a quotation here and there
- Organising an answer which explains what is happening in the text and giving quotations to support what you write

....

- Writing in such a way as to show that you have thought about the intentions of the writer of the text and that you understand the techniques used
- Writing at some length, giving your viewpoint on the text and commenting by picking out details to support your views
- Looking at the text as a work of art, demonstrating clear critical judgement and explaining to the reader of your essay how the enjoyment of the text is assisted by literary devices, linguistic effects and psychological insights; showing how the text relates to the time when it was written

The dotted line above represents the division between lower- and higher-level grades. Higher-level performance begins when you start to consider your response as a reader of the text. The highest level is reached when you offer an enthusiastic personal response and show how this piece of literature is a product of its time.

Coursework Set aside an hour or so at the start of your work to plan
essay what you have to do.

- List all the points you feel are needed to cover the
  task. Collect page references of information and
  quotations that will support what you have to say. A
  helpful tool is the highlighter pen: this saves
  painstaking copying and enables you to target
  precisely what you want to use.
- Focus on what you consider to be the main points of
  the essay. Try to sum up your argument in a single
  sentence, which could be the closing sentence of your
  essay. Depending on the essay title, it could be a
  statement about a character: Despite being absent
  through much of Maya's childhood, Mother does
  provide her daughter with encouragement,
  understanding and support in her teenage years; an
  opinion about a setting: The contrast between the
  repressive southern states and the more liberal
  northern ones is a recurring feature; or a judgement
  on a theme: Throughout the novel Maya Angelou
  demonstrates the long-term, damaging consequences
  of early insecurity and a sense of displacement.
- Make a short essay plan. Use the first paragraph to
  introduce the argument you wish to make. In the
  following paragraphs develop this argument with
  details, examples and other possible points of view.
  Sum up your argument in the last paragraph. Check
  you have answered the question.
- Write the essay, remembering all the time the central
  point you are making.
- On completion, go back over what you have written
  to eliminate careless errors and improve expression.
  Read it aloud to yourself, or, if you are feeling more
  confident, to a relative or friend.

If you can, try to type your essay using a word
processor. This will allow you to correct and improve
your writing without spoiling its appearance.

Examination essay

The essay written in an examination often carries more marks than the coursework essay even though it is written under considerable time pressure.

In the revision period build up notes on various aspects of the text you are using. Fortunately, in acquiring this set of York Notes on *I Know Why the Caged Bird Sings*, you have made a prudent beginning! York Notes are set out to give you vital information and help you to construct your personal overview of the text.

Make notes with appropriate quotations about the key issues of the set text. Go into the examination knowing your text and having a clear set of opinions about it.

In most English Literature examinations you can take in copies of your set books. This is an enormous advantage although it may lull you into a false sense of security. Beware! There is simply not enough time in an examination to read the book from scratch.

In the examination

- Read the question paper carefully and remind yourself what you have to do.
- Look at the questions on your set texts to select the one that most interests you and mentally work out the points you wish to stress.
- Remind yourself of the time available and how you are going to use it.
- Briefly map out a short plan in note form that will keep your writing on track and illustrate the key argument you want to make.
- Then set about writing it.
- When you have finished, check through to eliminate errors.

To summarise, these are keys to success

- **Know the text**
- **Have a clear understanding of and opinions on the storyline, characters, setting, themes and writer's concerns**
- **Select the right material**
- **Plan and write a clear response, continually bearing the question in mind**

SAMPLE ESSAY PLAN

A typical essay question on *I Know Why the Caged Bird Sings* is followed by a sample essay plan in note form. This does not present the only answer to the question, so do not be afraid to include your own ideas, or exclude some of the following. Remember that quotations are essential to prove and illustrate the points you make.

What have you learned about racial prejudice in America in the 1930s and 1940s from reading *I Know Why the Caged Bird Sings*?

Introduction Place the novel in context – young girl growing up in different places: Stamps, St Louis, Los Angeles, San Francisco. Brief historical background – slavery, Civil War, Reconstruction, Ku Klux Klan (see Context & Setting in Part One of these Notes).

Part 1 Novel is **autobiographical** (see Literary Terms) – reader sees things through Maya's eyes, both as a child and as an adult. As a child Maya is very conscious of her colour – longs to be white, does not always understand prejudice around her and is often offended by it (white girls' attempts to mock Momma) – sometimes envious of lifestyle of Whites – regards them as alien beings.

Part 2 Focus on individual incidents in Stamps, showing what they reveal about racial prejudice:
- The presence of the Ku Klux Klan (Chapter 3) demonstrates: arrogance of whites through the sheriff; the fear in which the Ku Klux Klan are held through the reaction of Momma and Uncle Willie
- The behaviour of the white children to Momma (Chapter 5) demonstrates: the power even white children held over Blacks; the powerlessness of Blacks to fight back – Momma's victory is due to her passive not active resistance

- Mrs Cullinan's attempt to rename Maya (Chapter 16) demonstrates: the arrogant assumption that this was a reasonable thing to do; the acceptance of this by Miss Glory; the difference between Momma's passive and Maya's active resistance
- The revival (Chapter 18) demonstrates: the acceptance by the Blacks of their situation, combined with the need to believe that things would change
- The World Championship fight (Chapter 19) demonstrates: the perception of the conflict between Black and White as a fight; the pride the Blacks have in being victorious over the Whites; the fear they have of reprisal
- The graduation ceremony (Chapter 23) demonstrates: the inequality in educational provision; the superior attitude of the white Mr Donleavy; the lowly expectations imposed on the Blacks; the importance of the Negro National Anthem in reviving spirits
- The visit to the dentist (Chapter 24) demonstrates: the extreme and ugly nature of racial prejudice
- The body in the pond (Chapter 25) demonstrates: the acceptance of such brutal behaviour by the adults (Momma and Uncle Willie); the bewilderment of the child (Bailey) in the face of such blatant hatred

Part 3 San Francisco, in many ways, was more enlightened than the South. Maya learns to feel at home there and has a positive educational experience at the George Washington High School despite her view that San Franciscans were 'sadly mistaken' (p. 207, Chapter 27) in their view that racism was absent from the city. Evidence of racism to be found in: Mr Red Leg's story where the success of the scam depended on the white man's prejudiced perception of Blacks; Maya's prolonged fight to work on the San Franciscan streetcars.

Conclusion   Reader's perceptions obviously strongly influenced by
                 authorial viewpoint. Maya Angelou writing story with
                 hindsight and after extensive involvement in Civil
                 Rights Movement. Nevertheless clear evidence is given
                 of extreme racial prejudice in the southern state of
                 Arkansas, and in the northern state of California
                 though less pronounced.

FURTHER QUESTIONS

Here are more questions on the novel. Work out what
your answer would be, always being sure to draw up a
plan first.

1 Trace the changes in the relationship between Maya
   and her brother Bailey over the course of the story.
2 Write about the importance of education and
   learning in Maya's formative years.
3 To what extent was Maya's life affected by her
   traumatic experience of rape at the age of eight?
4 Write about the importance of religion in the story.
   It may help you to think about:
   • Momma's views on religion
   • Reverend Howard Thomas
   • The revival
   • Maya's fears of damnation
5 What similarities and differences are shown
   between Stamps and St Louis?
6 To what extent does Maya Angelou impose her
   adult ideas on the story of her childhood?
7 In Chapter 7 when Maya writes about Momma she
   says 'I saw only her power and strength' (p. 45).
   How are her power and strength shown to the
   reader through:
   • the things she does
   • the things she says
   • her affect on other people?

8 What evidence is there to suggest that Maya was a difficult and very confused teenager?

9 Write about the importance of Maya's father in the story.

10 What have you learned about the black community in Stamps in the 1930s from reading this story?

11 'displacement is the rust on the razor that threatens the throat'. Write about the concept of displacement as revealed in the story.

12 Choose three of the following characters: Uncle Willie, Mrs Flowers, Mrs Cullinan, Miss Kirwin. Write about the part they play in Maya's life and the way she feels towards them.

13 'In San Francisco, for the first time, I perceived myself as part of something' (p. 206, Chapter 27). Explain why the city held such a strong attraction for Maya.

14 'A fascinating and very complex character'. To what extent do you think this description fits Maya's mother? Give reasons for your answer.

15 Would you recommend this book to a friend? Give reasons for your answer outlining what you consider to be the book's strongest and/or weakest qualities.

PART FIVE

CULTURAL CONNECTIONS

BROADER PERSPECTIVES

An understanding of slavery is helpful if you are to understand the situation of the Blacks in *I Know Why the Caged Bird Sings*, particularly those living in Stamps, Arkansas. Many slaves wrote or dictated accounts of their experiences of legal bondage in the southern states. These accounts are known as slave narratives. The only one known to be written by a woman is Harriet Jacob's *Incidents in the life of a Slave Girl* which was published under the pseudonym of Linda Brent in 1861.

Other novels which deal with some of the issues raised in *I Know Why the Caged Bird Sings* are *To Kill a Mockingbird* (1960), written by a white woman called Harper Lee and set in the southern state of Alabama, and *Roll of Thunder, Hear My Cry*, by Mildred Taylor, which depicts the struggle of the Logan family to survive in the racist southern state of Mississippi.

You might also find interesting *The Color Purple* (1982), by Alice Walker, a sensitive and touching novel, written in the form of a series of letters, detailing the life of Celie and set in the Deep South between the wars. *The Color Purple* is also a highly successful film, produced by Steven Spielberg.

Finally, having read this book, you might like to read its sequel *Gather Together in My Name*, or try one of Maya Angelou's collections of poetry such as *Just Give me a Cool Drink of Water 'Fore I Diiie* or *Shaker, Why Don't You Sing?*.

aphorism a short, snappy saying expressing a general truth

autobiography an account of a person's life as written by that person

bildungsroman a novel which describes a character's development from childhood to maturity, focusing on their experience, education and identity

chronological order events arranged in the correct sequence of time

colloquial a local or informal type of speech

episodic divided into or composed of episodes

first-person narrative the narrator speaks of herself as 'I' and is generally a character in the story. This differs from the third-person narrative in which the narrator describes the characters as 'he', 'she' or 'they'

personification the giving of human characteristics to inanimate objects or ideas

simile when one thing is said to be like another, allowing a comparison to be made

structure the overall principle of organisation in a work of literature

style the characteristic manner in which a writer expresses herself, or the particular manner of an individual literary work

TEST ANSWERS

TEST YOURSELF (Chapters 1–8)

A 1 Uncle Willie *(Chapter 2)*
••• 2 Mr Steward *(Chapter 3)*
3 Maya *(Chapter 4)*
4 Momma *(Chapter 5)*
5 Reverend Thomas *(Chapter 6)*
6 Momma *(Chapter 8)*
7 Uncle Willie *(Chapter 2)*
8 Ku Klux Klan *(Chapter 3)*
9 Momma *(Chapter 5)*

TEST YOURSELF (Chapters 9–13)

A 1 Momma *(Chapter 9)*
••• 2 Father *(Chapter 9)*
3 Bailey *(Chapter 10)*
4 Mr Freeman *(Chapter 11)*
5 Mr Freeman's lawyer *(Chapter 13)*
6 Grandmother Baxter *(Chapter 13)*
7 Mother *(Chapter 10)*
8 Maya's uncles *(Chapter 10)*
9 Mr Freeman *(Chapter 12)*

TEST YOURSELF (Chapters 14–24)

A 1 Mrs Flowers *(Chapter 15)*
••• 2 Mrs Cullinan *(Chapter 16)*
3 Bailey *(Chapter 17)*
4 Tommy Valdon *(Chapter 20)*
5 Mr Taylor *(Chapter 22)*

6 Dentist Lincoln *(Chapter 24)*
7 The black congregation *(Chapter 18)*
8 Joyce *(Chapter 21)*
9 Mr Donleavy *(Chapter 23)*

TEST YOURSELF (Chapters 25–29)

A 1 Bailey *(Chapter 25)*
••• 2 Mother *(Chapter 26)*
3 Mother *(Chapter 26)*
4 Black on streetcar *(Chapter 27)*
5 Daddy Clidell *(Chapter 29)*
6 Mr Red Leg *(Chapter 29)*
7 Bailey *(Chapter 25)*
8 Momma *(Chapter 26)*
9 Miss Kirwin *(Chapter 28)*

TEST YOURSELF (Chapters 30–36)

A 1 Father *(Chapter 30)*
••• 2 Dolores *(Chapter 31)*
3 Maya *(Chapter 31)*
4 Maya *(Chapter 32)*
5 Bailey *(Chapter 33)*
6 Mother *(Chapter 34)*
7 Father *(Chapter 30)*
8 The homeless children
   (Chapter 32)
9 The youth Maya seduces
   (Chapter 35)

NOTES

Notes

GCSE and equivalent levels (£3.50 each)

Maya Angelou
I Know Why the Caged Bird Sings

Jane Austen
Pride and Prejudice

Harold Brighouse
Hobson's Choice

Charlotte Brontë
Jane Eyre

Emily Brontë
Wuthering Heights

Charles Dickens
David Copperfield

Charles Dickens
Great Expectations

Charles Dickens
Hard Times

George Eliot
Silas Marner

William Golding
Lord of the Flies

Willis Hall
The Long and the Short and the Tall

Thomas Hardy
Far from the Madding Crowd

Thomas Hardy
The Mayor of Casterbridge

Thomas Hardy
Tess of the d'Urbervilles

L.P. Hartley
The Go-Between

Seamus Heaney
Selected Poems

Susan Hill
I'm the King of the Castle

Barry Hines
A Kestrel for a Knave

Louise Lawrence
Children of the Dust

Harper Lee
To Kill a Mockingbird

Laurie Lee
Cider with Rosie

Arthur Miller
A View from the Bridge

Arthur Miller
The Crucible

Robert O'Brien
Z for Zachariah

George Orwell
Animal Farm

J.B. Priestley
An Inspector Calls

Willy Russell
Educating Rita

Willy Russell
Our Day Out

J.D. Salinger
The Catcher in the Rye

William Shakespeare
Henry V

William Shakespeare
Julius Caesar

William Shakespeare
Macbeth

William Shakespeare
A Midsummer Night's Dream

William Shakespeare
The Merchant of Venice

William Shakespeare
Romeo and Juliet

William Shakespeare
The Tempest

William Shakespeare
Twelfth Night

George Bernard Shaw
Pygmalion

R.C. Sherriff
Journey's End

Rukshana Smith
Salt on the snow

John Steinbeck
Of Mice and Men

R.L. Stevenson
Dr Jekyll and Mr Hyde

Robert Swindells
Daz 4 Zoe

Mildred D. Taylor
Roll of Thunder, Hear My Cry

Mark Twain
The Adventures of Huckleberry Finn

James Watson
Talking in Whispers

A Choice of Poets

Nineteenth Century Short Stories

Poetry of the First World War

Six Women Poets

Advanced level (£3.99 each)

Margaret Atwood
The Handmaid's Tale

William Blake
Songs of Innocence and of Experience

Emily Brontë
Wuthering Heights

Geoffrey Chaucer
The Wife of Bath's Prologue and Tale

Joseph Conrad
Heart of Darkness

Charles Dickens
Great Expectations

F. Scott Fitzgerald
The Great Gatsby

Thomas Hardy
Tess of the d'Urbervilles

James Joyce
Dubliners

Arthur Miller
Death of a Salesman

William Shakespeare
Antony and Cleopatra

William Shakespeare
Hamlet

William Shakespeare
King Lear

William Shakespeare
The Merchant of Venice

William Shakespeare
Romeo and Juliet

William Shakespeare
The Tempest

Mary Shelley
Frankenstein

Alice Walker
The Color Purple

Tennessee Williams
A Streetcar Named Desire

Jane Austen
Emma

Jane Austen
Pride and Prejudice

Charlotte Brontë
Jane Eyre

Seamus Heaney
Selected Poems

William Shakespeare
Much Ado About Nothing

William Shakespeare
Othello

John Webster
The Duchess of Malfi

Chinua Achebe
Things Fall Apart

Edward Albee
Who's Afraid of Virginia Woolf?

Jane Austen
Mansfield Park

Jane Austen
Northanger Abbey

Jane Austen
Persuasion

Jane Austen
Sense and Sensibility

Samuel Beckett
Waiting for Godot

Alan Bennett
Talking Heads

John Betjeman
Selected Poems

Robert Bolt
A Man for All Seasons

Robert Burns
Selected Poems

Lord Byron
Selected Poems

Geoffrey Chaucer
The Franklin's Tale

Geoffrey Chaucer
The Merchant's Tale

Geoffrey Chaucer
The Miller's Tale

Geoffrey Chaucer
The Nun's Priest's Tale

Geoffrey Chaucer
Prologue to the Canterbury Tales

Samuel Taylor Coleridge
Selected Poems

Daniel Defoe
Moll Flanders

Daniel Defoe
Robinson Crusoe

Shelagh Delaney
A Taste of Honey

Charles Dickens
Bleak House

Charles Dickens
Oliver Twist

Emily Dickinson
Selected Poems

John Donne
Selected Poems

Douglas Dunn
Selected Poems

George Eliot
Middlemarch

George Eliot
The Mill on the Floss

T.S. Eliot
The Waste Land

T.S. Eliot
Selected Poems

Henry Fielding
Joseph Andrews

E.M. Forster
Howards End

E.M. Forster
A Passage to India

John Fowles
The French Lieutenant's Woman

Brian Friel
Translations

Elizabeth Gaskell
North and South

Oliver Goldsmith
She Stoops to Conquer

Graham Greene
Brighton Rock

Thomas Hardy
Jude the Obscure

Thomas Hardy
Selected Poems

Nathaniel Hawthorne
The Scarlet Letter

Ernest Hemingway
The Old Man and the Sea

Homer
The Iliad

Homer
The Odyssey

Aldous Huxley
Brave New World

Ben Jonson
The Alchemist

Ben Jonson
Volpone

James Joyce
A Portrait of the Artist as a Young Man

John Keats
Selected Poems

Philip Larkin
Selected Poems

D.H. Lawrence
The Rainbow

D.H. Lawrence
Sons and Lovers

D.H. Lawrence
Women in Love

Christopher Marlowe
Doctor Faustus

John Milton
Paradise Lost Bks I & II

John Milton
Paradise Lost IV & IX

Sean O'Casey
Juno and the Paycock

George Orwell
Nineteen Eighty-four

John Osborne
Look Back in Anger

Wilfred Owen
Selected Poems

Harold Pinter
The Caretaker

Sylvia Plath
Selected Works

Alexander Pope
Selected Poems

Jean Rhys
Wide Sargasso Sea

William Shakespeare
As You Like It

William Shakespeare
Coriolanus

William Shakespeare
Henry IV Pt 1

William Shakespeare
Henry V

William Shakespeare
Julius Caesar

William Shakespeare
Measure for Measure

William Shakespeare
Much Ado About Nothing

William Shakespeare
A Midsummer Night's Dream

William Shakespeare
Richard II

William Shakespeare
Richard III

William Shakespeare
Sonnets

William Shakespeare
The Taming of the Shrew

William Shakespeare
The Winter's Tale

George Bernard Shaw
Arms and the Man

George Bernard Shaw
Saint Joan

Richard Brinsley Sheridan
The Rivals

Muriel Spark
The Prime of Miss Jean Brodie

John Steinbeck
The Grapes of Wrath

John Steinbeck
The Pearl

Tom Stoppard
*Rosencrantz and Guildenstern
are Dead*

Jonathan Swift
Gulliver's Travels

John Millington Synge
*The Playboy of the Western
World*

W.M. Thackeray
Vanity Fair

Virgil
The Aeneid

Derek Walcott
Selected Poems

Oscar Wilde
*The Importance of Being
Earnest*

Tennessee Williams
Cat on a Hot Tin Roof

Tennessee Williams
The Glass Menagerie

Virginia Woolf
Mrs Dalloway

Virginia Woolf
To the Lighthouse

William Wordsworth
Selected Poems

W.B. Yeats
Selected Poems

York Notes – the Ultimate Literature Guides

York Notes are recognised as the best literature study guides.
If you have enjoyed using this book and have found it useful, you
can now order others directly from us – simply follow the ordering
instructions below.

HOW TO ORDER

Decide which title(s) you require and then order in one of the following
ways:

Booksellers
All titles available from good bookstores.

By post
List the title(s) you require in the space provided overleaf,
select your method of payment, complete your name and
address details and return your completed order form and
payment to:

> *Addison Wesley Longman Ltd*
> *PO BOX 88*
> *Harlow*
> *Essex CM19 5SR*

By phone
Call our Customer Information Centre on 01279 623923 to
place your order, quoting mail number: HEYN1.

By fax
Complete the order form overleaf, ensuring you fill in your
name and address details and method of payment, and fax it
to us on 01279 414130.

By e-mail
E-mail your order to us on awlhe.orders@awl.co.uk listing
title(s) and quantity required and providing full name and
address details as requested overleaf. Please quote mail
number: HEYN1. Please do not send credit card details by
e-mail.

York Notes Order Form

Titles required:

Quantity	Title/ISBN	Price

Sub total _____

Please add £2.50 postage & packing _____

(P & P is free for orders over £50) _____

Total _____

Mail no: HEYN1

Your Name _____

Your Address _____

_____

Postcode _____ Telephone _____

Method of payment

☐ I enclose a cheque or a P/O for £_____ made payable to Addison Wesley Longman Ltd

☐ Please charge my Visa/Access/AMEX/Diners Club card
Number _____ Expiry Date _____
Signature _____ Date _____

(please ensure that the address given above is the same as for your credit card)

Prices and other details are correct at time of going to press but may change without notice. All orders are subject to status.

☐ *Please tick this box if you would like a complete listing of Longman Study Guides (suitable for GCSE and A-level students)*

York Press

Longman

Addison Wesley Longman